To Orb Bowling,

Hope you ENJOY The memories!

Mike Edwards
" The Greenfield Gunner "

Don't Give Me the Scores, Just the Stories

Tales from the Ray Mears Era and More

by

Mike Edwards

author HOUSE™

1663 LIBERTY DRIVE, SUITE 200
BLOOMINGTON, INDIANA 47403
(800) 839-8640
WWW.AUTHORHOUSE.COM

First published by AuthorHouse 10/13/05

ISBN: 1-4208-6221-9 (sc)

Printed in the United States of America
Bloomington, Indiana

This book is printed on acid-free paper.

This book is dedicated to my late father Robert Edwards and my mother Louise Edwards who loved the game of basketball and who were the inspiration for all that I have ever achieved; to my wife Debbie and son Brett; to Coach Ray Mears; to all the Volunteer basketball players who gave the University of Tennessee some of the best years of their lives; and to all the loyal Tennessee fans who just like a story.

Table of Contents

Acknowledgments

This book exemplifies a team effort as the following people made major contributions to its development.

I would like to thank Patsy McCulley for all her tireless work in helping to prepare this book. Without her patience and endless hours of typing and editing, my dream of publishing this work would never have become a reality. Also, much appreciation is expressed to Amy Ridge who designed the front and back covers and whose computer expertise "saved the day" many times as she solved many technical problems.

I am grateful to Coach Ray Mears for the many hours we spent talking Tennessee Basketball. I will always cherish the time we spent together.

I would also like to thank the former players who contributed. Without their stories this book would never have materialized; to name a couple: Bill Justus who has always been very loyal to the UT Basketball Family for some extra services I asked him to do, and also to Skip Plotnicki who provided numerous tales from Coach Mears' early years at the University of Tennessee.

A special thanks to Bud Ford and the UT Sports Information Department for permission to use the basketball pictures in this book. The photographs, in enhancing the reality of the stories, heighten the reader's nostalgia for that period of time.

A Word From the Author

During the 1960's and early 1970's, University of Tennessee basketball reached a level of excellence that placed the program among the nation's round ball elite. The Vols had an inspirational coach in Ray Mears who created a new excitement in basketball "on the hill." He orchestrated the pageantry of Hollywood on the court combining a basketball tradition with "show biz" along with a new winning attitude. The UT band, students, cheerleaders, and the community were all a part of Coach's basketball extravaganza; everyone was a star in his show. Tennesseans eagerly anticipated the next game in the confines of Stokely Center as a family and community spirit prevailed.

Mears operated his program with class as the All-American appearance was exhibited by his players and coaching staff. Even the atmosphere within Stokely was "spit shined" on game nights to represent the wholesomeness that Americans admired. Players— representing their communities, their families, and, above all, Ray Mears and the basketball program at the University of Tennessee— understood no misbehavior was tolerated.

The players acquired a quality education at UT, and they received a second degree from Ray Mears who taught them to deal with adversity, the importance of hard work and discipline, and a great respect for authority. They practiced together, ate together, traveled together, won together, lost together, and, like it was all a dream, left the University to begin their careers. But all of them today retain the learning experiences gleaned from Ray Mears, and his influence emerges in the personalities of many of his players. Billy Justus, a former All-American, once said, "If I could ever play again, there would be only one coach I would want on my bench and that would be Ray Mears." When Billy made that statement, he spoke for all of us.

A lot has been written about Ray Mears and the basketball excellence he attained while at the University of Tennessee, but only a few young men have had the rare opportunity of participating in his program. This book is a behind-the-scenes look at what it was like to perform for one of the greatest basketball coaches of all time as seen through the stories told by his former players.

Ray Mears—the ringmaster; Ray Mears—the showman; Ray Mears—the miracle worker; or Ray Mears—the salesman. Pick any of these descriptions of the man who directed the Vols, and they all describe the coach that led Tennessee to some of the most successful years in basketball. *Don't Give Me the Scores, Just the Stories* portrays life under the "Big Top" when Tennessee basketball players experienced some of the best years of their lives.

Foreword

Each year thousands upon thousands of loyal University of Tennessee fans journey to Knoxville to watch "Big Orange" football and basketball. In the fall, the color around Neyland Stadium can be as spectacular as the autumn foliage that blazes in the Smoky Mountains.

UT fans are interested only in one team—the Volunteers from the University of Tennessee; the "gladiators" in orange and white are their pride and joy. UT football tradition includes the Tennessee walking horse strutting around the green "battlefield" lined in white, the team running through the giant "T," the Pride of the Southland playing *Rocky Top,* the Vol navy making their way along the Tennessee River, and John Ward bellowing "Give him six, touchdown, Tennessee!" The world at Neyland Stadium on a crisp, sun-lit fall afternoon is filled with excitement and glamour.

Most fans would relish an opportunity to be a player in such a fine tradition. What could be more gratifying than performing before thousands of people in the largest football facility in America. One loyal "Big Orange" supporter found his love for the University of Tennessee and its football program so immense that he donated one million dollars for the opportunity to run through the "T" with the team.

As a former basketball player, I have always been fascinated with "Big Orange" football fans even though I played the sport that used a ball that was much more easily handled and a game in which you did not have to fight the elements since you played indoors. The glitter and hype on fall afternoons; the fans making their way to the stadium wearing various styles of orange attire; and tailgating, an excuse for partying—such is UT football, a way of life for Tennesseans in the fall.

In the 1960's and early 70's there was another game on "the hill"—a game that challenged football for recognition and tradition— "Big Orange Basketball." In fact, there would be no "Big Orange" anything if it had not been for a basketball coach by the name of Ray Mears. He brainstormed the concept while on a recruiting trip in Ohio where he noticed a lighted billboard, which read "Marlboro Country." The rest is history. "Big Orange Country" was born not with the life-blood of Tennessee football but from a sport and coach on the rise—basketball. The idea came not from a southerner, but from a coach reared on northern soil. Thompson-Boling arena stands as a testament to the outstanding job Ray Mears did at the University of Tennessee. His influence on a community and his players will withstand the test of time.

Enticed fans flocked to the Ray Mears show by the thousands as Stokely Athletic Center was transformed into an atmosphere that resembled Ringling Brothers Circus. The UT Pep Band marched around the floor, the team went through Harlem Globetrotters' style drills to the tunes of *Sweet Georgia Brown* and *Cotton Candy*, and a player by the name of Roger Peltz performed while juggling three basketballs and riding a unicycle simultaneously. A Big Orange paraded around the court; majorette and cheerleader showgirls were galore. The Orange Tie Club, a group of supporters seated across from center "ring," gave their all for the "big circus." As a gigantic flag was unfurled from the top of the arena, lights were dimmed and a color guard stood their ground. A huge "T" provided an imposing entrance for the "circus" performers to run through, and a large spotlight focused on them as they entered the "Big Top."

Victor and Gus were seated in the "Big Top" and ready to give the officials a "warm" reception; while on the opposite end sat stately UT President Andy Holt all clad in orange, leaving little doubt for whom he would be rooting. High on the "Big Top" was the "Voice of the Vols," John Ward, who had to do a "high wire act" across a catwalk before he could announce, "It's basketball time in Tennessee"; and later, when that orange-suited Volunteer performer hit that first long jumper, Ward's voice would vibrate across the Tennessee plateau with "Bottom!" Country music stars performed at the half, and even the wrestling of a bear brought mountaineers to the show. There was more color and excitement than one could imagine. Oh, for the years under the "Big Top!"

Coach Mears preferred the selling of cotton candy and candied apples under the "tent." But the administration did not always buy into the circus theme; thus, hot dogs and popcorn were the main treats under the "Big Top." Coach Mears proposed the building of a giant, rotating-lighted basketball several hundred feet above the arena to draw fans to the "main event," but the idea never materialized, due to the possibility of disrupting air traffic.

With all the excitement and glamour, the years under the "Big Top" were short indeed, and former players find it difficult to understand why the "circus" could not stay in town. But the "ringmaster" retired from the game and the "circus closed down." We wait patiently but the remembrances of the past are slowly disappearing as the years move forward. There seems to have never been a "circus" quite like this one—a show with all the glitter and pageantry of yore. What made this "circus" spectacular was Coach Ray Mears, the "ringmaster" that won over 70 per cent of his games and had enough All-Conference and All-American players to challenge one of the greatest basketball programs in the land and its "Baron."

It was a time when Tennessee basketball was one of "The Greatest Shows on Earth!"

Roger Peltz during pre-game warm-ups

Life Is a Circus With Every Story an Act in Itself

The Circus Parade

The Circus!—The Circus!—The
throb of the drums,
And the blare of the horns, as the
Band-wagon comes;
The clash and the clang of the cymbals
that beat,
As the glittering pageant winds down
the long street!
In the Circus parade there is glory
clean down
From the first spangled horse to the
mule of the Clown,
With the gleam and the glint and the
glamour and glare
Of the days of enchantment all
glimmering there!
And there are the banners of silvery
fold
Caressing the winds with their fringes
of gold,
And their high-lifted standards, with
spear-tips aglow,
And the helmeted knights that go
riding below.
There's the Chariot, wrought of some
marvelous shell
The Sea gave to Neptune, first washing
it well
With its fabulous waters of gold, till
it gleams
Like the galleon rare of an Argonaut's
dreams.
And the Elephant, too, (with his undulant
stride
That rocks the high throne of a king
in his pride),
That in jungles of India shook from
his flanks
The tigers that leapt from the Jujubee-
banks.
Here's the long, ever-changing, mysterious

line
Of the Cages, with hints of their glories
divine
From the barred little windows, cut high
in the rear
Where the close-hidden animals' noses
appear.
Here's the Pyramid-car, with its splendor
and flash,
And the Goddess on high, in a hot-
scarlet sash
And a pen-wiper skirt!—O the rarest
of sights
Is this "Queen of the Air" in Cerulean
tights!
Then the far-away clash of the cym-
bals, and then
The swoon of the tune ere it wakens
again
With the capering tones of the gallant
cornet
That go dancing away in a mad
minuet.
The Circus!— The Circus!— The throb
of the drums,
And the blare of the horns, as the
Band-wagon comes;
The clash and the clang of the cymbals
that beat,
As the glittering pageant winds down
the long street.

James Whitcomb Riley
The Hoosier Poet

Tennessee Signs the "Barnum of Basketball"

Ringling Brothers' P. T. Barnum once said, "Give them something different and they'll be back." Throughout the 1960's and early 70's the University of Tennessee basketball program had a "ringmaster" that put P.T.'s philosophy on the basketball court. His name was Ray Mears. He brought the "Big Top" to Knoxville, Tennessee, and there it stayed for over a decade and a half.

There were rally girls, a band that paraded around the court, a basketball-juggling player, country musicians that performed at half time, and a fearless player that wrestled a bear. The basketball entertainers wore orange and white striped warm-up pants and dazzled Tennesseans with their pre-game ball handling wizardry. Yes, this "circus," in town on most Saturday and Monday nights, would have made P.T. Barnum proud.

At center stage was Coach Ray Mears and that's just where he wanted to be. He also brought his own theme—Big Orange Country—and promoted it with orange everywhere in the arena. "Mears, the Coach"; "Mears, the Competitor"; "Mears, the Disciplinarian"; "Mears, the Innovator"; and "Mears, the Motivator"—many sportswriters have described him with great accuracy, but he may best be remembered as "Mears, the Showman." There have been national championships won at the University of Tennessee in various sports; but the color, glamour, and salesmanship of the Mears Era would be hard to surpass. For all of us who played on the team or viewed the games as a spectator, it was a special time, and we all knew we were involved in something totally unique.

The "circus" almost did not come to town. Mears had been coaching at Wittenberg College, a Division III school in Ohio, in the latter 1950's and had done a superb job. He had won a Division III NCAA Championship, and major schools were beginning to take notice. As the University of Tennessee basketball program had

5

fallen on hard times, the Athletic Department was thinking change. On staff were Jim MacDonald, who had coached Volunteer football, and Bowden Wyatt, who had also coached football and had assumed athletic director responsibilities due to General Bob Neyland's illness.

In discussing a basketball coaching change with Wyatt, Coach MacDonald recommended a fellow Ohioan, Ray Mears, as a possible candidate. Coach Wyatt advised MacDonald to invite Coach Mears to Knoxville. At that time, the U.T. basketball season was still in progress and the year was going poorly. Wyatt informed MacDonald to keep the visit quiet and out of the media since the coach at the time, John Sines, had not been dismissed.

Upon his arrival to Knoxville, Coach Mears, lodged on one of the upper floors of the Andrew Johnson Hotel, prepared for a meeting with Coach Wyatt and Coach MacDonald that evening. Clad in a coat and tie, he awaited their call in his room.

Around seven o'clock there was a knock on the door, and MacDonald and Wyatt both dressed in casual clothes entered. Since the coach of the U.T. basketball program had not been dismissed, Bowden Wyatt informed Mears that he was to disclose to no one his purpose for being there. Then Wyatt told Mears that he was their choice to be the next basketball coach at the University of Tennessee but the hiring would be dependent on a couple of factors: First, General Neyland would have to pass on because they did not think he would approve of building up the basketball program due to his loyalty to football; and, secondly, John Sines would have to be terminated.

They put the facts on the table, and Mears pondered the proposition carefully. His goal was to attain a major college position but perhaps the timing at Tennessee was not right at the present. With a statement informing the acting athletic director he would have an interest in the job if the factors materialized, Mears ended the initial contact with the University of Tennessee but not before being retained in his hotel room for the remainder of the visit and told to order room service.

Coach Mears came to Knoxville thinking the decision would be made to name him coach of the Volunteers; instead, his coaching career was put on a tightrope with a wait and see future. Mears was ready to move up in the college ranks, and timing was very important in finding a major college job. He left Knoxville with doubts in his mind on the Tennessee possibilities.

Several months passed and Coach Mears was entertaining plans of going to the University of Denver to further his career. Just when he thought he was headed west, he got the call from Tennessee. Wyatt and MacDonald wanted to talk further. They told him the General had passed on and they were prepared to let Coach Sines go.

Mears traveled to Knoxville and met with Wyatt and MacDonald again. This time there was no secrecy. Bowden Wyatt offered Coach Mears the Head Basketball job. He accepted and pulled out his pen to sign the contract. Bowden Wyatt looked at Coach Mears and said, "Son, we don't have contracts; we do everything down here with a handshake." Coach just looked at him in dismay. Seeing that Coach was uncomfortable, Wyatt pulled out a napkin, wrote the salary on it, signed it, and pushed it across the table for Mears to endorse.

The rest is history. One of the greatest basketball coaches of all time committed to the Tennessee Vols on a napkin.

Green Jell-O

A typical game day menu for basketball at the University of Tennessee during the Ray Mears Era was supposedly based on nutritional studies which would give the athlete optimal performance precisely during game time. At noon the team would be fed a large steak, baked potato, green beans, salad, hot rolls and iced tea. At 4:00 in the afternoon, the menu changed drastically. Approximately four hours before game time the squad was served oatmeal cookies, milkshakes, and green Jell-O. Carbohydrates ruled the late afternoon meal.

During the famous Ray Mears pre-game talk, the Volunteers would be compared to "gladiators" who went into the arena as the Romans did centuries before and emerged exalted, victorious, and worthy of the highest praise or on their shield, defeated and humiliated. I do not know what the Romans ate before battle, but I would bet my Tennessee orange blazer it was not milkshakes, oatmeal cookies, and green Jell-O. The energy theory might have made sense, but the truth of the matter was that before game time most players could not hear Coach's final remarks because their stomachs were growling.

It is my understanding that Bernard King, not buying into the pre-game theory on at least one occasion, ordered a shrimp cocktail sent to his hotel room to satisfy his hunger. On another occasion, a Tennessee player was caught eating a hot dog at the concession stand by the coaching staff. Penalties for eating after pre-game could be stiff, especially if the Vols came out on the losing end.

The Vols in Athens, Georgia, before playing the Bulldogs, had finished the milkshakes and oatmeal cookies, and were waiting on the green Jell-O. Most players did not eat much of the Jell-O, perhaps because it always looked like a cross between green slime and rubber. On this particular day the waitress was late delivering the gelatin; however, she finally came through the door, much to our disappointment, with the meal topper. On a tray was the most beautifully cut orange Jell-O I had ever seen. Being so proud of his product, the hotel manager made an appearance to take some of the credit. As the waitress held the tray high, the manager looked at Coach Mears and told him in honor of the Vols they had made wonderful orange Jell-O.

The poor guy barely finished speaking when Coach Mears was on him like a dog on meat. When the Vol mentor got this certain look in his eyes, you just did not want to be around him, and he had that look all over his face. That poor waitress and manager took the tongue lashing of their lives. Mears adamantly informed the restaurant manager he had ordered green Jell-O, that is what he expected, and the squad was not leaving until the request was met. The manager tried to explain that they had no green Jell-O and the orange was only available because they had special ordered it. Mears, livid at this point, told the poor guy that this team would wait until it arrived, that is, if he expected to be paid. The manager told Coach they would have to go to the grocery store to get green Jell-O and have it prepared; it would take time. The team waited one and one-half hours on that Jell-O. Everybody took one or two of the usual bites and left.

I really have not cared much for Jell-O since those days. In fact, I have eaten it only a few times, usually when I have been sick. I discovered that day why it had to be green. When Coach Mears won a national championship at Wittenberg College in Ohio, they served green Jell-O for the pre-game meal. He had insisted it be served for every pre-game meal thereafter. The green gelatin was considered superstitious good luck. We did beat Georgia that night and it was an extremely close game. At the post-game press conference most coaches would have emphasized that it was this play or that play that made the difference, but Coach Mears would have probably said it was the green Jell-O and explained how important it is to be patient.

Is He Dead?

The last year Adolph Rupp coached, he spoke at our season-ending banquet that was held at the conclusion of my junior year. I really did not want to go hear him speak; in fact, looking at him at the time made me a little sick at my stomach.

We had a great basketball team that year, winning nineteen games; but all our dreams came crashing down when Kentucky beat us in the last game of the season, which tied us with the Cats for the championship. Since they had beaten us by two points in Lexington and one point in Knoxville, they got to go to the NCAA tournament and we stayed home.

During my three years of eligibility, we could have won the conference three straight years; however, a play here and a play there kept us from all those dreams, and Kentucky was the team responsible. This past season was the Baron's last and I guess that fate played a part. Nevertheless, by today's standards, we would have been in the NCAA tournament three consecutive years. During my basketball career, I was very fortunate to have come in contact with two of the greatest coaches to have ever taught the game—Adolph Rupp and John Wooden. I played against Rupp, and Wooden recruited me at UCLA. Just being in the presence of those two coaches would have been the ultimate dream for many athletes, and for me the opportunity has been two of my most cherished sports memories.

During his oration at the banquet, Rupp talked about the heated rivalry he had with Babe McCarthy, who had been a superb coach at Mississippi State. McCarthy had coached a lot of great players, but one of his best was Bailey Howell who later had a stellar career with the Boston Celtics. The Bulldogs had been a thorn in Kentucky's side for many years, beating them on several occasions.

On a cold winter's night, Rupp's Cats having defeated Vanderbilt were in the locker room preparing to head back to Kentucky when the president of the school came in and called Coach Rupp to a corner to inform him of bad news from Starkville, Mississippi. The

Associated Press had reported that Babe McCarthy had died of a stroke after the Bulldogs' game.

Unresponsive to the shocking news, Rupp remained silent while the president moved to another part of the locker room. Adolph stood in the corner of the room for a few minutes with his arms folded across his chest, staring at the wall, and then he moved slowly back toward the president. He grabbed the president's arm and told him that he would like to fly to Mississippi State for the funeral. The impressed president then took Adolph's right hand and told him that he thought it was a gracious gesture for him to go to Mississippi and pay his respects to Coach McCarthy. Rupp replied, "Respects, hell, I'm going down there to make sure they put the S.O.B. in the ground."

Well, fortunately for the Mississippi State fans, the Associated Press report was false and Adolph and Babe continued to battle each other on the courts for many more memorable games.

Win One for the Rupper

I played in Memorial Coliseum on the Kentucky campus four years, and I have only a few fond memories while competing there. We challenged the Cats tough the three years we were fighting for the Southeastern Conference Championship but lost all three games in Lexington by close scores. In fact, less than five points decided two games. The arena had a capacity of 10,500 fans, and the seats came right down to the playing floor, leaving little room on the side court. The place vibrated with noise, and to most teams it could be very intimidating.

Since I had played high school basketball in Indiana, I was used to gyms with a lot of noise; nonetheless, Kentucky had a real snake pit atmosphere, and the students took full advantage of it. Their remarks and insulting chants could upset the most self-confident teams and coaches. Even though the memories on the Cats' floor were not at the top of my list of my most enjoyable experiences, the stories were.

During my junior year at Tennessee, we had completed a week of preparation and were on our way to play Kentucky. Indiana and Kentucky have always been big rivals; and being from Indiana, it was a game I looked forward to and wanted a victory badly. .

The news out of Lexington was one of gloom. Coach Rupp was sick. He had been diagnosed with gangrene in his leg, and there was rumor his leg would have to be amputated in order to save his life. A good Tennessee basketball team was coming to town, and the head on the snake was ill. Every report in the newspapers emphasized just how ill Coach Rupp was and that prayers were needed. Our team did not have any trouble saying a prayer for him, but we still wanted to beat him in the worst way. For me it was a border grudge; Hoosiers mix with Kentuckians about as well as oil and water.

Everything had gone great the day of the game. The pre-game meal was a brunch because the game was to be regionally broadcast at 1:00 p.m. Coach Mears had given a great motivational talk on the national importance of beating Kentucky and how if we won we would remember it until the day we died. I do not think our team had ever been more prepared to play.

As we took the floor to warm up, there was a pall in the arena. It was hard to explain how the whole place took on a somber atmosphere. Each player occupied his appropriate position; both teams were warming up; the cheerleaders were in their place; the sportscasters and reporters were there in force; and the coaches were seated. There was one thing missing however; Rupp's seat was vacant. No one was sitting in his chair. *The Star-Spangled Banner* was played; *My Old Kentucky Home* was played. The starting lineups were introduced. Everything was set to go.

As we were receiving final instructions from Coach Mears, the most unbelievable roar I have ever heard by a crowd erupted. My eyes left our huddle and focused on the far part of the gym. Two Kentucky players were wheeling Adolph Rupp into the arena in a wheelchair. His heavily bandaged leg was stretched out straight and elevated slightly to aid circulation; a blanket had been placed over his legs and waist; and, yes, he had a brown suit on. The unrelenting crowd would not cease cheering as students were yelling and hugging each other. It was the most amazing tribute I have ever seen for anybody. The doctors advised the "Baron" not to go to the game because a blood clot could form, move from his leg to his heart and kill him. But I guess Adolph figured if he had to die, it might as well be on Bluegrass soil.

I do not know how much coaching the Baron did that day, but when they rolled him into Memorial Coliseum on that cold, March afternoon, that game belonged to Kentucky!

He Fouled Out on One Play

When playing at Kentucky, one could always count on a few constants: Adolph Rupp would be on the bench; the game would be a sellout; and Ralph Stout would be calling the game. When Ralph's path and mine would cross after I began my coaching career, I asked him why he was always assigned to officiate the Tennessee/Kentucky game, and he would just smile at me. Then I would usually make some remark like, "Did they give you season tickets?" or "Are you and Adolph related?" Ralph Stout was one of the best officials to ever call the game, and I was glad to have been able to spend some time with him. But to this day, it is still a mystery why he officiated the Tennessee/Kentucky games every year in Lexington.

Adolph Rupp could "work" a referee as well as Bob Knight, and most officials became undaunted to the degree they ignored him, dismissing his criticism as just a typical occurrence. I think players, coaches, and officials were all more thick-skinned back in the 60's and 70's. "Getting on" somebody was all just part of the game.

In one particular contest, I believe it was during the A.W. Davis years at Tennessee, Rupp had been particularly hard on the officiating crew due to the game being a little closer than he would like. According to Ralph Stout, who, of course, was the official, an aggressive play had taken place on a rebound; and Adolph quickly came off the bench, blasting Stout for not calling a foul on a Tennessee player who had been aggressively pursuing the ball. The Baron yelled, "Stout, blow your whistle; number 50 has just fouled out on that one play. I counted five fouls on him trying to get that one rebound. He should be out of the game. Blow your whistle and at least get one right. You hear me?" Ralph immediately blew his whistle, went straight at the Baron, and signaled a firm technical foul. Stout, with deep satisfaction, then remarked, "I believe I got this one right!"

Who's in Charge?

During my sophomore season as we headed on to the court to play the Cats, we got a warm reception. As we approached mid-court before a television audience, the student section pelted us with oranges. They came from all directions, splattering the floor and making a mess.

The Kentucky Athletic Director got on the microphone and tried to get the students to stop, but a second wave of fruit surged from the stands. I honestly do not believe there was one orange left in the entire state of Kentucky after those students finished throwing them at us. After the A.D. spoke to no avail, the President of the University attempted to get the incident to cease, and a third wave of oranges plummeted to the floor.

Finally, Coach Adolph Rupp took the microphone and in his authoritative manner warned: "The next student who throws an orange out of the stands I am personally going to throw you out of this school." I'm telling you that arena was like a morgue as you could have heard a pin drop. In fact, some of the students even volunteered to assist in the clean up.

In Kentucky, when the Baron spoke, people listened!

Call Home

It is my understanding that Adolph Rupp could be an extreme disciplinarian and a tough taskmaster when it came to the game of basketball. Mears was like that at Tennessee; Woody Hayes at Ohio State and Joe Paterno at Penn State were similar.

According to Kentucky players, Rupp was set in his ways. The uniforms they wore were not flashy—plain blue and white with no frills. When in Knoxville, most teams stayed in the Hyatt, but Rupp housed his teams at the outdated Andrew Johnson Hotel downtown. Adolph, usually reserving a room on a separate floor from the players, stayed up most of the night, visiting with reporters and telling stories. Many of these stories were related over a glass of Kentucky Bourbon. Rupp in Knoxville was an "event."

He was quick to praise his players, but many times he would expel his wrath in an attempt to motivate them to improve. On one occasion a Kentucky player, as the story goes, had not been playing to his potential or practicing as hard as he should. Rupp stopped practice, dropped a dime at the player's feet, and told him to call home and have his parents come and get him. He was through as a Kentucky player. The coach wanted no part of mediocrity. Rupp's teams were always extremely disciplined and very physical. They played hard with reckless abandon and were a mere image of their coach, rarely beating themselves. On one occasion after losing in the first round of the NCAA tournament, Rupp told a national television audience, "I was prepared to play but my team had different ideas."

After a hard fought game, the legendary Kentucky announcer Cawood Ledford was interviewing Rupp and remarked that one of his players had a great night by scoring 21 points. To the amazement of Ledford, Rupp replied, "Great hell, his man scored 27, so in my book he was minus 6."

When Kentucky forced Coach Rupp to take the mandatory retirement required by state law, it was a sad day, not just for Kentucky but for all lovers of the game of basketball and especially Tennessee fans who would never again see the "man in the brown suit" on the sidelines of Stokely Center.

Beef and "The Broom"

 At five feet and a few inches, plus one hundred and fifty pounds dripping wet, stood Assistant Coach Stu Aberdeen, better known by his nickname, "Beef." And, yes, he was named after livestock. I have no idea who gave him the name, but that is what most of the players called him when I arrived at Tennessee. Stu Aberdeen was one of the most dedicated basketball coaches I have ever been around. The man could work twenty-four hours without sleep and still work some more. He had the metabolism of a hummingbird and a caring heart. He was the most likable guy you would ever want to meet off the court, but he could be demanding on the practice floor.

I miss Coach Aberdeen. I can still feel his right hand reaching up and clasping the back of my neck and recall those concerned words coming out of his mouth, "Hey, big guy, how's your mum and dad?"

Coach Aberdeen's official title at UT was Associate Basketball Coach. He was in charge of drilling the post players in practice and designing the Vol defense. If he had been a football coach, he would have been the defensive coordinator and would have loved the linemen. Aberdeen respected physically tough kids. He had no patience for wimps and people who went against the status quo. He was partial to players who came from the inner city of large metropolitan areas; and if they were sons of cops, firemen or construction workers, the mold was perfect. Aberdeen believed tough kids came from tough areas. If you were the son of a banker or lawyer and were part of the country club set, living in a nice home and having a comfortable life, he had a name for you, "Cake Eater."

Aberdeen was a blue-collar coach and one of the best. He could demote a player physically and mentally and then rebuild him to compete with the elite in the southeastern conference. His tactics made us mature faster and helped us to realize that life and basketball were not all fun and games.

One of Coach Aberdeen's favorite drills was to take an old worn out broom, cover the bristles with a towel, wrap it in tape, and then hit the players with the broom in order to improve their shooting concentration. A three-man weave up the court, an outside jumper by Len Kosmalski and a whack on the elbow—the bruise didn't heal on the 7'0" center for three months. You could expect to be hit in the face, chest, legs, feet, or back—no area of the body was exempt. Some players' chests were so red they looked like they had spent a day on the beach with no sunscreen. It was tough, but, oh, the satisfaction when that ball got nothing but net and Aberdeen would yell, "That a way, big guy!" Thank goodness, Coach Aberdeen was around for a time that made men from boys and lessons were taught in a more liberal manner.

Coach Aberdeen passed away in his early forties, much too young for a great coach and a fine person. I miss the conversations with him when he tried to help a twenty-year-old kid improve his self-confidence, telling him that he could accomplish anything he set out to do. I miss his smile. Gosh, if he were around today, I'd even let him come into my classroom and take his best shot with that broom to the back of my head.

The Buckets

One experience that players did not relish at Tennessee was pre-season practice, which was held in the fall. During the Mears Era the coaching staff were going through the Lombardi stage. You know everybody goes through stages: we wear our hair long, and we change to short; we wear bright-colored clothes, and we change to drab colors; we buy station wagon vehicles, and we change to sports cars. Well, anyway, Vince Lombardi of the Green Bay Packers was "in," and the U.T. coaching staff decided to incorporate his philosophy as a part of their program.

Lombardi time meant you arrived at 1:50 p.m. for a 2:00 p.m. scheduled team meeting. You dressed and presented yourself in a clean, wholesome manner, known as the All-American look— clean-shaven, short hair, and neat clothes. You exhibited class at all times.

If coaches required their squads to follow this strict regimen today, perhaps players would complain they were being deprived of their right to individuality. The biggest difference between the Lombardi program and today's attitude is that Lombardi stressed the team concept, whereas today the focus is on individual showmanship. During Mears' day at Tennessee a sign in the locker room reminded players: "There is no 'I' in 'TEAM.'" If you did not follow that belief, you were selfish; and there was no place for selfish players wearing orange.

Coach Stu Aberdeen obtained possession of the pre-season program Lombardi used at Green Bay and adapted it to fit Vol basketball needs. Rumor had it that he actually traveled to Green Bay to get it, but no proof is available. Stu's philosophy was that a player had to "hurt big before he could win big." The program consisted of thirty minutes of 3-on-3-basketball, followed by a mile-and-a-half run on the track for time, and then another forty-five minutes of tough agilities in the gym. A player not making the mile-and-a-half run in the allotted time reported to the track the next day at 5:00 a.m. to make up the time. Some players were such lousy runners, that every fall they ran enough miles to take them back to their hometown. The best times for make up runners were on foggy mornings as they would cross the inside of the track unnoticed by a coach doing the timing. Unfortunately, for these early risers there were not many "smoky mountain" mornings.

During his strenuous agility session, Coach Aberdeen placed buckets conveniently around the court so that the players could throw up if the urge developed. Lloyd Richardson, setting the record for the most regurgitations in one day, threw up three different times, filling three buckets. We thought he was a goner; he could have vomited a fourth time, but there just was not anything left in his system. Lloyd's misfortune gave his teammates a reprieve when Coach Aberdeen would go to him and cheer him on with one liners, such as: "That a way, Lloyd, show us your guts; you gotta have guts to play this game; that a way, big guy, are you finished? You're holding everybody up."

I can hardly look at a paint bucket today without picturing Lloyd all bent over, losing his innards.

Flossing Teeth

On the road, when the Tennessee Volunteers practiced the night prior to their game, the Coaches and squad shared the same locker room. Players did not make a habit of watching coaches change their garments; however, Coach Aberdeen was the price of admission. His baggy boxers went on first; they usually had some design on them that Ringling Brothers Circus would have envied. After that he put his black nylon knee-length socks on, and then came his huge black wingtip shoes. Next was a white sleeveless undershirt. At this point all he needed was a camera and he would have looked like a northern tourist on the streets of Gatlinburg.

Flossing teeth was not "in" back in those days; brushing and fluoride were the general rule. Coach Aberdeen was way ahead of his time when it came to dental care. On several occasions in practice he was seen pulling a thread out of his sock using it to floss his teeth. He was good at it, too; he always got exactly the right size and thickness. He worked it good in the front and then the sides; then he would put the string in his pocket and follow up by moving his tongue all around.

Could this have contributed to Coach Aberdeen pristine teeth and winning smile?

Pistol Pete on Sportsmanship

During the Mears Era, the Vols competed against arguably the greatest guard to ever have played college basketball, "Pistol" Pete Maravich. Pete played for his dad at LSU and was a scoring machine. He was a showman and a master magician with the basketball; making passing an art, he put the ball behind his back, through his legs, around his neck, or whiplashed it from hand to hand. Receiving his passes was an ordeal in itself as he hit guys in the head, the back, and the stomach.

When "Pistol" Pete came to Knoxville, the "show" was always a sellout and a hot ticket. His scoring average was consistently over forty points per game, but when he played the Vols, they always managed to hold him in the twenties. Mears and Aberdeen would play a box and one on him, meaning the defense would play zone on all the other players and one Vol would guard Maravich man-to-man. This defense plus the Vols' deliberate offensive style limited Pete's scoring. During his entire career at UT, Billy Hann, one of the best defensive guards and playmakers to ever wear the orange and white, guarded Pete.

In his final game against Maravich in Stokely, Hann was doing another splendid job of holding Maravich's scoring down when he picked up his fifth personal foul. As he went to the bench and sat down, he happened to look up. Pistol Pete had followed him to the bench and had bent over, appearing to say something to Hann. The crowd sensed a show of sportsmanship from "The Pistol" and began to stand and applaud.

After the game, Marvin West, a sportswriter for the *Knoxville News-Sentinel*, stopped by the locker room to interview Hann. The first question he asked was: "After you fouled out, that was a great show of sportsmanship by Pete Maravich to come to the bench and shake your hand, especially since you have held him down in scoring for the last three years. What did he say to you?" Billy responded, "He called me a no good son of a bitch and he hoped to never see my ugly face again as long as I lived."

Several years later Billy Hann, passing Pete in an airport terminal, tried to talk to him; but Pete, still remembering Hann's tenacious defense, refused his amicable approach.

How'd You Like To Bite My...?

During the 1972-73 season we were in a heated battle for the Southeastern Conference Championship with Kentucky, and the season boiled down to the last game in Lexington. The winner would take all. We always practiced on the opposing team's court the day before the game, and this trip was no different. But as we pulled up to Memorial Coliseum, I knew that this was not just another game; it was going to be for number one.

When we arrived at the main entrance, I could not believe my eyes as Kentucky students were lined up four and five deep around the arena. Although the temperature was zero with several inches of snow on the ground, these students were not permitted in the gym for twenty-four hours. At the time, all seats for Kentucky students for basketball games were first come, first serve. Huddling in tents and around campfires, these students were going to appreciate their seats on game night.

For the Vols it was the finale to another outstanding year. We were tied for first place and with a win over the Cats we would claim a Southeastern Conference Championship. For Lloyd Richardson, Eddie Voelker, Larry Robinson, and me, it would be the last time we would don an orange jersey. The year before I had been voted Most Valuable Player in the Southeastern Conference along with Honorable Mention All-American status and had followed that up this year by being selected once again to the All-Southeastern Conference team. All my dreams had come true, and now all I wanted for the Vols was an outright SEC Championship.

As we got off the bus a chant started with the students. Kentucky students were always good at chanting; maybe it is in their religion up there. But, anyway, I had put one foot on the pavement upon leaving the bus and I heard this: "Edwards, Edwards, how'd you like to bite my ass?" And as I got closer to the door, the chant got louder, "Edwards, Edwards, how'd you like to bite my ass?" It was all I could do to keep from laughing; it was hilarious. As we entered the inside of the building, most of the team was laughing, and I think Larry Robinson said, "Don't worry about it; they really love you."

I could not even avoid the verbal harassment in the locker room as several teammates were standing on benches chanting, "Edwards, Edwards, how'd you like to bite my ass?" I will have to say it was one of the most relaxed and loose practices we had at Tennessee, removing the usual pre-game jitters.

Of all the stories, I think my wife Debbie has enjoyed this one the most. During our years of marriage there were times when she would get upset with me and, unfortunately, I would hear that chant again, "Edwards, Edwards, how'd you like to bite my . . .?"

Go To . . ., Tennessee

During my freshman season we were scheduled to play a religious junior college in East Tennessee. This squad had an outstanding program and the Tennessee freshmen were probably their most bitter rivals.

Not eligible for varsity competition, freshmen played a twenty-five game schedule in preparation for the "big time" next year. All the home games were played prior to the varsity game in Stokely and always drew a good crowd.

On this particular trip to the church-related institution Vol Coach A.W. Davis must have had some concern because he gathered the squad in the locker room the day before the contest and lectured us on proper manners. He went into this spiel about the school's ethics, stating that a Protestant denomination had founded the college and emphasized a need to exhibit a deep respect for the players. After A.W. finished, I thought, boy, this is going to be a tough night—no cussing, no nothing. He also told us we would have to play our best game because this was what their team lived for—to beat Tennessee.

As the bus approached the gym, there appeared to be a riotous commotion. Students were yelling and screaming while displaying derogatory signs, and the driver had a hard time maneuvering the chartered coach around them. Coach Davis led us off the bus, and the student chants intensified: "Go to hell, Tennessee, go to hell! Go to hell, Tennessee, go to hell!" Good people—religious school? You've got to be kidding! These fans wanted our blood.

Well, the Vols gave the non-secular squad the respect A.W. demanded and then proceeded to "beat the living tar out of them."

Hand Grenades

Coach Mears, one of the greatest motivational speakers of all time, could fire his team up in a second. One pre-game speech was titled "Run for the Roses," and he talked about horses in the Kentucky Derby and how they all run to be number one with only one horse being the champion. He concluded by handing a rose to a certain player and saying, "That's what this game tonight is all about—being number one. We are running for the roses!"

Another motivational speech Coach would give involved the Indy 500. He talked about the bravery of the drivers and how they strove to be the winner of the greatest race in the world. Winning the 500 meant having an image of their face engraved on the Borg-Warner Trophy, symbolizing their racing immortality. This was a race with thirty-three drivers but only one champion. There was always this quest to be number one with Coach Mears. His whole basketball philosophy revolved around it. But none of the speeches matched the one we got before each Mississippi State game. For three years straight he gave the same speech and the same story. I know it by heart.

Mississippi State had a player on their team who was a Vietnam War veteran and, according to Mears, one tough character. During the war, a Viet Cong threw a grenade into the foxhole the veteran was in; and, instead of running like hell, he picked the loaded bomb up with his bare hands and threw it back at them. When Coach talked about him picking it up with his bare hand, his face would get red, his eyes became as large as saucers, and spit would emit from his mouth. He would raise his left hand and scream, "He picked it up with his bare hand; boys, that's who you're playing tonight. This boy had no fear of a grenade or dying. Do you think he's going to be afraid of the Big Orange?" Mears would shout: "What courage, determination, loyalty, and love of country this player has!" With his hand raised high in the air, finally, he would end by saying, "We are going to have to play our best game ever—no mistakes."

Tennessee won the game and Coach Mears' motivational scheme was successful. The fearless Mississippi State war veteran, who showed great heroics on the battlefield, was a non-factor as his only participation was during the warm ups.

The Fruit Basket

During my freshman year the coaching staff scheduled a fall scrimmage at Davidson College. In recent years, Davidson had been a very good basketball team coached by Lefty Dreisel who stated he left "to make Maryland the UCLA of the East." His successor was a young coach by the name of Terry Holland, who later coached at Virginia. Being my first road trip, I was especially excited, as I would be competing against Joe Sutter who was a freshman at Davidson and played on the Indiana All-Star team with me that previous summer.

It was a long journey to Davidson, and the fact the coaching staff decided to take a bus rather than fly made it even longer. Before we left Coach Mears met with the team admonishing them that this was a "business trip" and the scrimmage would be treated as if it were a regular season contest.

However, upon boarding the bus a group of varsity players decided to pass the time by playing cards. A trunk was laid flat, nickels and dimes came out of pockets, and cards were dealt. The game livened up and the noise got louder. Mears kept turning around in the front of the bus and looking back. Eddie Voelker who was sitting beside me remarked, "This isn't good." About the time he said that here came Coach Mears, and he was not a happy trooper. He had the look of taking no prisoners as he flipped over the trunk with cards and coins spilling everywhere. The tongue lashing those guys received rivaled the fury of the items flying through the air. That bus was quiet the rest of the trip because everybody knew Coach was in charge, and there was no question regarding the purpose for heading to Davidson.

If you think the fireworks were over, hold on to your seats. As the bus pulled under the overhang at the motel and stopped, the resident manager came out of the motel with the most gorgeous fruit basket I had ever seen complete with an orange bow on it. In the middle of the basket was a fifth of Jack Daniels whiskey. There was a note attached and Mears opened it. Enclosed was a card from

Terry Holland, the coach at Davidson, which read: "Hope you enjoy your stay here."

An unpleasant trip to this point, had taken a turn for the worse. Coach slammed the basket down and remarked, "Who does he think I am? I don't drink." He looked toward the back of the bus and yelled, "Boys, get a good nights sleep; you better be ready to play tomorrow." I can tell you there was fire in those words.

I was one of the last players off the bus, and behind me was the team manager. He took one look at that fruit basket, put his arm around it, and said, "Coach doesn't drink, but I've been known to take a nip or two." And he hauled the prize to his motel room.

The next day both teams won their scrimmages and the trip home was less eventful.

A Cherry of a Test

Over the years we have all heard and read about academic scandals that have taken place on university campuses. Some of these scandals have hurt the integrity of colleges and certainly the respect of athletic departments. I've been asked many times if any classroom improprieties ever occurred at Tennessee during my tenure. Well, that is a tough question which over the years I have avoided answering; but since this is a book about stories, now is a good opportunity to respond.

Typically on a weeknight, tutors came to the athletic dorm to assist athletes who were having difficulties in a particular subject area. The session schedules were posted on the lobby elevator door. I utilized these provisions quite extensively my freshman year, as they were an invaluable aid in preparing for an exam. Usually, the tutor gave to the athletes practice tests, which gave a fairly good indication of the difficulty of the official exam that would be administered.

Like a lot of athletes, I was enrolled in "Wild" Bill Cherry's Economic Geography class. He had scheduled a massive multiple-choice final exam, and I decided along with a lot of other athletes that a tutoring session was in order. Nothing was different the night of the session; old tests were brought in as study guides, and I felt prepared for the next day's exam. However, when I got the exam the next day, I was not prepared for what I saw.

The tutor had inadvertently brought the exact test for us to use as practice. There were one hundred and sixty questions and every one of those suckers hit. I was not even reading the questions; I was just marking answers. I was filling in question sixty-five and the studious girl seated next to me was still on number ten. This test was long and hard. I looked at teammate Lloyd Richardson, and he just smiled and shook his head. Point guard Eddie Voelker whispered, "Can you believe this?" I was finished in ten minutes. I looked around the room, and most all the athletes had finished. Feeling guilty about the situation, I went back and changed nine answers so I would not get a perfect score.

The next day when we got to class, Bill Cherry lived up to his nickname. He was "Wild." The average score on that test was seventy-eight, but the average score for the athletes was ninety-seven, thanks to the several football players who got one hundreds. Cherry thought someone had stolen the test. After the air cleared, we explained to Dr. Jimmy Walls, head of the Geography Department who was a good friend of Dr. Cherry, that the proctor had mistakenly brought the actual test to the athletes' practice session and the situation was resolved.

Boerwinkle or Bullwinkle?

When Coach Mears was recruiting me to play basketball for the Vols in 1969, my younger brother, John, was in elementary school at the time. As was the practice with most college coaches in the recruiting process, they would bring a book of photographs that depicted the academic side of the school as well as the athletic. Ole Miss was an exception. When their coaches visited, they brought a book that contained all the beauty pageant winners and the Miss Americas that had attended Ole Miss. Perhaps that is what convinced Johnny Neumann, the much-heralded Tennessee prospect, to sign with the Rebels. Some coaches also brought a game film of their team for the prospect to view.

On this particular visit to my home Coach Mears had brought both his recruit book and a game film. During his book presentation, he kept repeating that Boerwinkle was in the film he had brought in hopes that our family would be excited when seeing him play. My brother John, captivated with Coach Mears' talk about Boerwinkle (mistakingly assuming Coach had said "Bullwinkle"), asked him if he really had a film of Bullwinkle. Coach Mears lit up like a Christmas tree and said, "You know Boerwinkle?" To which John replied, "I sure do; I watch him all the time."

Coach was really impressed with this young man knowing all about Boerwinkle and even said, "Our recruiting and promotion must really be paying off up here in Indiana if young kids know all about Boerwinkle." My brother could hardly sit still through the rest of Coach Mears' presentation and kept asking, "Man, can we see Bullwinkle now? I want to see Bullwinkle!" Coach Mears, unable to delay him any longer, set up the screen and the 16mm projector and turned on the film. He was not five seconds into the film of the Volunteers playing when my brother John got up out of his seat and shouted, "This is not Bullwinkle! I thought we were going to see Bullwinkle; this is not even a cartoon." The stunned Coach Mears replied: "John, this film has our 7'0" All-American center Tom Boerwinkle in it. Tom plays for the Chicago Bulls." John, shaken with disappointment and unimpressed with the Bullwinkle impersonator, just turned and headed upstairs to play with his toys.

You're in the Game

During the 1972-73 season, Mississippi State came to play the Vols in Knoxville as the Southeastern Conference schedule got under way. State's program was a little down, but they were still a hard team to beat in Starkville. On this particular night, the game was to be held in the friendly confines of Stokely Center, and as usual the arena was packed.

Eddie Voelker, who was a reserve point guard, experienced a night he probably would like to forget. Coach Mears was set on using seven players in a game, and he seldom went any farther down the bench. Voelker had not played much in the first one-fourth of the season and figured this night would not be any different. Eddie was from Kentucky and one of the best defensive players I have ever been around. He enjoyed every minute of making life miserable for offensive players in practice.

Assuming on this night that he was not going to get to play, he left his game jersey hanging in his locker. He put on his outer warm-up and the inner warm-up shirt. Perhaps he felt if he was not going to see action, he might as well be comfortable. The arena could get hot on game nights.

As the game was a blowout with about six minutes to go, Coach Mears signaled for Eddie to go into the game. I was not there to hear what Eddie told coach, but you can imagine telling the most organized, fiery and disciplined coach in the entire universe that you could not go into the game because you forgot your jersey.

Death Defying Act

 One of the most death defying acts ever witnessed occurred during the 1972 pre-season practice. The feat would have been "center ring" at Ringling Brothers. Coach Aberdeen had decided to take the basketball team to the Student Aquatic Center; and as a demonstration of mental toughness and courage, we were required to leap from the high dive into the deep end of the pool. Most players felt comfortable with the drill since they had access to public pools, although they were somewhat apprehensive with the height.

The player that had a major problem was Larry Robinson, our fine high post player who could not swim. Aberdeen unaware of Larry's aquatic handicap rallied the players up the ladder toward the tower.

As they reached the top of the board, the team could sense Larry was quite uneasy. All of the players took their turn, and Larry decided he would go last. Aberdeen must have been informed that Robinson could not swim, so Coach went to the opposite end of the pool to seek assistance from Ray Bussard, the Vols' swim coach. Coach Bussard immediately blew his whistle and summoned a group of his swimmers to the deep end. Then Aberdeen looked to the top of the tower and yelled, "Okay, big guy, be tough; we're ready." Larry must have appreciated that encouragement since he was the one standing thirty feet up with nothing but bottom below.

Larry finally worked up enough courage to jump. The 6'5" post player weighed over two hundred pounds and was solid muscle, fitting the mold of a football player rather than basketball player. Larry was like a massive boulder when he hit that water, and, like a boulder, he went straight to the bottom. Bussard wasted no time. He blew his whistle and an all out rescue ensued. Any delay might have resulted in a recovery. If that pool had not had a bottom, Larry would still be going down. Well, Larry Robinson gained a lot of respect from his teammates that day, but what was really important to him was that he was still alive.

Fire in the Chemistry Building

In reviewing my class schedule in the fall of my junior year, Dr. Andy Kozar, the physical education department head and my advisor, informed me that I would need to enroll in a chemistry class. I was shocked. I had no chemistry background as I did not take the course in high school, and labs and hospital emergency rooms have always had an intimidating effect on me. I tried to explain to Andy that I had completed three quarters of geology that should fulfill my science requirement. He informed me that geology was not an alternative and if I wanted to graduate I better get mentally prepared to tackle chemistry.

The first day of lab was a disaster, and the school is fortunate the building is still there. Tommy, my instructor, who was a rather large individual, assumed that his students had some background of a chemistry lab, but this "Hoosier" certainly did not. I looked at all those test tubes, wires hanging down, and other apparatus; I knew this had to be Dr. Frankenstein's abode. The environment and also the people around me who looked quite gifted intellectually intimidated me. It appeared to me that all the students were wearing dark-rimmed glasses and were in the Einstein category.

Before we even got started, I spilled hydrochloric acid on the student to the right. Wiping the chemical off did not help much as holes started emerging in his jeans, and I can tell you that holes in jeans were not "in" then.

Next, "Big Tommy" said, "Open the lab manual to page 1, turn your Bunsen burner on, and begin to work on lab Assignment A." Not knowing what a Bunsen burner was, I was in trouble from the start. There was a girl next to me who was a full-blooded flower child. She had long, waist-length hair; tank top; no bra; beads around her neck; blue jeans with a rope belt; no socks with sandals; and peace sign earrings. I did figure out, however, what the Bunsen burner was by watching her. With great hesitation I turned the knob marked "gas" counter-clockwise where it could turn no further and lit the Bunsen stick.

What happened next was better than watching any launch at Cape Kennedy. The flame shot up in seconds and ascended a good twenty to twenty-five feet directly into the lab ceiling, burning a nice hole. I did not know "Big Tommy" could move so fast. He was at my station in a flash, turning the gas knob clockwise as fast as his hand would operate. Man, I felt bad.

As I was walking out of class, "Big Tommy" yelled for me to wait up. I was still shaking from the incident, but he told me not to worry about it because tomorrow he would be better prepared. He would make sure that the Knoxville Fire Department, Unit for Hazardous Chemicals, and First Aid personnel would be present and located behind my workstation.

One for the Records

Upon my arrival at the University of Tennessee, one of the first players that I met was Lloyd Richardson from Rogersville, Tennessee. He had been an outstanding high school player and expectations were high for him on the U.T. campus, especially since he was a Tennessee boy. At that first meeting, Lloyd told me sports reporters labeled him the Rogersville Rifle and that he was "in the mold" of A.W. Davis, a great All-American basketball player in the 60's. Lloyd also announced his ambition was to work hard and possibly shatter some records.

Lloyd played a vital role in some of the Vol games, but he never surpassed any record on the court in his career; however, that all changed the night of the basketball banquet our senior year. Coach Mears and Coach Aberdeen initiated a new tradition that seniors would give a brief talk during the banquet on what the Tennessee basketball program had meant to them. Lloyd was scheduled to speak before me.

When Lloyd began his oration, I sensed I was in for a long wait. The Rogersville Rifle had a stack of note cards for his speech that was thicker than most textbooks. As he spoke and spoke and spoke some more, it seemed to me like night had turned to morning. Since I was next to speak, I was already nervous; and this delay made the palms of my hands sweat that much more.

Finally, Lloyd concluded. I don't know who was seated next to me, but I remember looking at them and saying, "Lloyd is in the record books now; that's the longest speech in the history of the Tennessee Vols Basketball Banquet."

How Do You Spell That?

Every fall a representative from the Athletic House in Knoxville came to the dorm to measure the basketball players for athletic apparel. The clothing varied from season to season; in the fall polo shirts and windbreakers were in style, and in the spring T-shirts and shorts were in vogue. All the clothing had "Tennessee Basketball" inscribed on it.

One fall a salesman came to the dorm selling windbreakers with "Tennessee Basketball" stamped on the front. The general procedure was to ask the player's name, take his measurement, and fill out the order form. When they came to our 7'0" center, Len Kosmalski, the process was interrupted. When taking the order, the salesman asked him, "What is your name?" The big center replied, "Len Kosmalski." The salesman began to write the order and then came to an abrupt stop. "Len Kosmalski, how in the hell do you spell that?" he asked. The big center cleverly replied without hesitation, "LEN!"

Making the Connection

During the '69-'70 season, a local radio station in Knoxville customarily broadcast Vol freshmen basketball games, giving fans a chance to follow the progress of future varsity players. Greenfield, Indiana, my hometown, had a local radio station WSMJ that would pick up the radio feeds from Knoxville, beginning with my sophomore year. But during my freshman year, the only way hometown fans could follow my career would be to travel to Knoxville or read about the game the next day in the local paper, that is, except for one local Greenfield family friend, Bill Dishman.

Bill worked for the Bell Telephone Company in Greenfield and devised an intriguing scheme. Thirty minutes before our freshman game, I called him from my dorm room at a number he gave me for the Bell Control Center in Greenfield. After we made contact, I was to dial my radio to the station on which the game was to be broadcast; I would then leave the radio beside the telephone receiver. Bill, listening to the entire game over the telephone, was always the first person in Greenfield to know the game's results. It was continually a mystery to my parents how he could obtain the information so quickly. (By the way, I was never charged for the call, thank goodness.)

The Haircut

During the 1972-73 season the Vols traveled to Marquette to play the powerful Warriors coached by the legendary Al McGuire. The Tennessee team was on an emotional high, having just beaten an outstanding South Carolina team in Knoxville coached by Frank McGuire. That Gamecock team had some outstanding players: Alex English, Kevin Joyce, and Brian Winters. The confident Vols were hoping to make it two in a row over the McGuires.

The Marquette game was a disaster. The Warriors, a very disciplined team, had lost only one or two games in their arena over the past several seasons. Their full-court press was so aggressive that we could not get the ball in-bounds. Vol players must have had eight assists in the game on in-bound passes, all to Allie McGuire, Al's son. We only scored thirty points which at the time was the lowest total ever for a Ray Mears coached team.

The highlight of the game occurred prior to tip off. After the national anthem and the introduction of players, Coach McGuire was asked to come to the center of the court, assuming he was to receive a plaque or recognition for a coaching milestone. However, the real reason he had been summoned to mid court was to give fans the opportunity to voice their opinions of the coach's new haircut. If the fans approved of the cut, they were to stand and cheer. Disapprovers would remain seated.

Much to his delight, the colorful Warrior's haircut overwhelmingly passed approval.

The Ketchup Bottle

The Vols had just finished their final practice in Philadelphia in preparation for a holiday tournament game against Villanova. The practice had not gone well, and the coaching staff was in a restless mood. Coach Mears called the team to the side and gave a thirty-minute speech on mental toughness, chastising the squad in regard to insignificant situations affecting their execution and performance. "The little things, the little things," he kept repeating it over and over. "The little things will frustrate you. The little things will get you beat." He also emphasized they can also win games for you. Diving for a loose ball in a key situation or grabbing a crucial rebound could be the difference in a win or loss. The talk seemed to go on and on.

Later that evening we were eating supper, and Stu Aberdeen, our energetic assistant coach, was seated across from me. Coach asked one of the players to pass the ketchup for his fries. As the ketchup bottle was brand new, he had trouble opening it. He grunted and moaned, trying to get the top to release, but it would not budge. The excitable mentor then banged the top with his fork. As he took another turn on the top, his face turned red and perspiration appeared on his forehead. After much effort, the top finally released, but it was obvious the bewilderment was mounting.

As Stu shook the ketchup bottle in the direction of his fries, no ketchup came out. He moved the bottle back and forth fiercely but with no success. Finally, in desperation, the feisty coach took his hand and slammed it against the bottom of the bottle; ketchup gushed on to his plate along with half the table and some of his clothes. Total frustration had now engulfed him.

Since I was sitting directly across from him, I could not resist seizing the moment to make a comment. I looked at Coach Aberdeen and said, "Don't let the little things upset you!"

White Trash

During his tenure at Tennessee, Ray Mears had a team depth of seven players. If a player was not among this elite group, his participation would be limited to pre-game warm-ups or if the contest was a blow out. Coach Mears had usually decided on his top five players the day pre-season pictures were taken; and if a squad member did not share a spot in a photo shot with the top seven players, he could expect to spend a long season on the bench because coach did not favor change.

Being one of the top seven players was never more important than on the trip to California to compete in the Trojan Classic against Southern Cal, Michigan State, and Houston during the 1970-71 campaign. At the time, every school was undefeated except Houston. Having beaten them in late November in Knoxville, we were again paired against them in this tournament. The Trojan Classic games would be the last contests before the Southeastern Conference schedule began; therefore, the tournament was crucial to the Vols in gaining momentum.

The Vols' team meeting held in the Century Plaza Hotel was like no other before or, for that matter, ever after. The plush meeting room would have met the approval of Donald Trump. The walls had satin wallpaper, and crystal chandeliers hung from the ceiling. Instead of sitting in rows, as was the norm, the squad was seated in luxurious chairs around a large walnut oval table.

Seated at the end of the table was Roger Peltz, a big part of our program during the pre-game warm-up drills. Riding a unicycle and juggling three balls simultaneously, Roger was a comedian, the team clown. He kept the squad at ease with his jokes and possessed a rare talent for imitating other people's voices. He could mimic Ed Sullivan, Gomer Pyle, SEC announcer Joe Dean, Howard Cosell, and even Stu Aberdeen of the Tennessee coaching staff. He was so talented in comedy that he later made it his life's work.

Roger, the headliner in the warm-ups, saw action only if the score was so lopsided there was no way the Vols could lose. If he did enter the game, he was a crowd favorite. Roger would electrify the fans by trying his best to score a basket; if he were fortunate enough to score a goal, Roger would merit a roar from the crowd equal to a game-winning shot.

As Mears and Aberdeen reviewed the game plan for the Houston Cougars, Peltz displayed no interest. The entire time the coaching staff spoke, Roger chewed gum and played with his gum wrapper, sometimes staring off into space. His demeanor proved he was not present mentally. Peltz assumed he was not going to see game action, so his attitude was "what the heck." Mears and Aberdeen, picking up on his nonchalant attitude, made no comments.

As the Tennessee Vols took the court that night in the Los Angeles Sports Arena, everything proceeded as planned until Roger Peltz began his unicycle performance. As he started to juggle the three balls, he lost his balance and fell head first to the floor. The fall was quite hilarious to the 10,000 spectators in attendance, especially since Roger had to struggle to get back on the unicycle due to the high seat. Even though it was more comical watching him attempt to board the one-wheeled apparatus than the actual fall, the coaching staff was not amused.

Losing the game down the stretch, the Vols expected an unpleasant post-game locker room scene. The players thought they would be criticized as a result of the missed free throws and errant shots that occurred during the last few minutes of the game, but Roger took that pressure off.

Coach Mears blasted Roger, criticizing him for not being on task during the pre-game meeting. He felt that due to Peltz's inattentiveness the 6'5" post player was unable to perform on the unicycle when the pressure was on. Mears, blaming Roger for the loss, said: "Peltz, we lost all our momentum when you fell off the unicycle and that cost us. We never recovered, and we lost the game."

Coach was not finished. When boarding the plane departing from California, the team was informed they would be flying to Mississippi State at Starkville to prepare for their first Southeastern Conference game against the Bulldogs. Coach Mears altered the scheduled plan for the squad to spend New Years Eve recuperating from the loss to Houston in a motel room; instead, the team spent that night on the practice floor.

44

Coach also placed his top seven players in first class on the plane while Roger and the remaining players were stationed in coach status. The top seven were served roast duck dipped in wine sauce while Roger's group munched on ham sandwiches. As a result of their second-class treatment, Roger and the other members of his group from that day forward nicknamed themselves the "White Trash." They wore white practice jerseys and rarely called each other by their surnames; they just addressed each other as "trash." The "trash" would never have been formed if Peltz had not fallen off the unicycle, but fate had it that way. Regardless, the guys developed a real friendship and respect for each other and certainly a reason to come to practice each day.

Halloween at Disneyland

On our trip to Los Angeles to play in the Trojan Classic during the '71-'72 season, Coach Mears arranged for the team to visit Disneyland. The dream of every kid in the 50's and 60's was to attend the park that Walt Disney created. There was no Disney World in Orlando at the time, so to see the "big mouse" you had to head west to California. For most kids growing up in the Midwest, going to California was like going to the moon; your chances of making the trip were zero to none. The trip to Disney was a dream come true.

Now the Volunteers were journeying to Disneyland for an evening of fun, or so they thought. Coach Mears decided to make the adventure a high profile night, meaning he wanted everyone at Disneyland to know what institution the team represented thereby requiring the squad to wear their traditional orange blazer, orange and black tie, and black pants. The Vols were highly conspicuous as they merited more stares than Mickey Mouse. Some confused tourists, unsure of what institution the Volunteers represented, asked if they were Texas Longhorns; others sarcastically queried if we were trick or treating or if we were from Pumpkin U.

Riding the different amusements proved to be uncomfortable to the team as their necktie kept flopping in their face. Some members of the squad felt they were there more for public relations than to have an enjoyable time. The orange blazer and black pants could have obviously been Halloween attire; but we were aware the trick or treat colors we sported really represented "Big Orange Country."

Choosing the Vols

I first met Coach Ray Mears and became familiar with the University of Tennessee upon entering my junior year in high school. Until that time I knew nothing about their basketball program, but I had heard of their fine football tradition.

In the fall of 1967 my high school coach, Joe Stanley, had been asked to speak at the Ball State University Coaches Clinic in Muncie, Indiana. The featured speaker that day was Ray Mears, the head basketball coach at the University of Tennessee.

During Coach Stanley's presentation, he requested that I come to the court and attempt a few jump shots from the top of the key. Unaware that I was to be part of the program, naturally I was quite nervous, but I headed for the floor. Without warming up, I hit nine straight and the tenth shot was in and out.

Immediately after the shooting display and without ever having seen me play in a high school game, Coach Mears approached me with an offering of a full basketball scholarship to the University of Tennessee. Informing me regarding his "star system," Coach stated that he recruited players to pass, players to rebound, and players to shoot. He encouraged me to come to UT to be a shooter.

A basketball coach at a major university had presented a full scholarship worth thousands of dollars to a player whom he had never seen perform for one second in an actual game situation. I do not know how many coaches would have taken that gamble, but this is one basketball player who was truly impressed.

Mears–the Motivator

Coach Mears was always at his prime when motivating teams before big games. In 1969 as a guest speaker at the Indiana All-Star Team banquet held in Greenfield, he delivered his famous battlefield speech. The Hoosier team was preparing to compete against Kentucky in the annual Indiana vs. Kentucky basketball classic that was played each summer. It was a two-game series. One game was played in Hinkle Field House in Indianapolis (14,000 fans) and the other in Louisville's Freedom Hall (19,000 fans). Both contests were sell-outs. To participate in these games, billed as the World Series of High School Basketball, was the dream of every player in Kentucky and Indiana.

Kentucky had beaten the Indiana All-Stars the last few years, and the Hoosiers were determined to turn the tables in 1969. The 1969 Indiana team was declared the finest in state history, and many fans still believe that today. The team boasted of four high school All-Americans: George McGinnis, Steve Downing, Billy James and Mike Edwards. The average scoring output was 25 points per player for the Hoosiers.

Coach Mears had come to Greenfield, Indiana, to speak to the team and motivate them in preparation for their contest against the Bluegrass Boys. It was at this banquet that the great orator delivered his famous battlefield story that reflected self-determination and perseverance. It was a speech that Mears utilized many times to fire up his Volunteer teams.

The story: Under enemy fire an American soldier was wounded on the battlefield in the Korean War, and his friend ran out to him. The wounded soldier looked up and said, "Go on; save yourself." To which came the reply, "I can't leave you; you're my buddy." He put the wounded soldier on his back and with tenacity said, "We're gonna run until we can't run no more, and then we're gonna walk until we can't walk no more, and then we're gonna crawl until we can't crawl no more, and then we're gonna get up and run some more."

Coach Mears emphasized that by manifesting the same determination and togetherness that the American soldier exhibited on the Korean battlefield, the Hoosiers could guarantee victories in their two games with the Kentucky All-Stars. Those words by Ray Mears provided the 1969 Indiana All-Star Team the inspiration needed to defeat Kentucky twice and become the most unselfish, talented team to ever play in the post-season classic.

Prostitutes and Goats

 Most of the athletes enrolled in "Wild" Bill Cherry's Economic Geography class, along with half of the University of Tennessee student body. He was entertaining and a master at telling stories. His lectures kept his students spellbound.

One tale he liked to relate was about goats that could climb trees on the Edwards Plateau in Texas. Most of the class was skeptical until he brought in some slides he had taken. Sure enough, goats were perched on branches in the tops of trees, but Dr. Cherry was unable to explain how the "billys" got up there. He had no pictures showing how they did it. Perhaps he just figured aliens had something to do with it.

On occasion, Dr. Cherry was known to take a "snort" or two and at times would use some salty language. After one class several girls, upset with his use of profanity, reported the embarrassing situation to Dr. Jimmy Walls who was Dr. Cherry's department head. Dr. Walls informed the females they did not have to endure Dr. Cherry's foul mouth and suggested that when he went into a cussing mode they should exit the classroom. He said Dr. Cherry would then get the message.

The next day the professor went into this spiel about South America having the highest prostitution rate in the world, and he got a little graphic with his remarks. The girls got up, per the advice of Dr. Walls, and headed for the door. Just before they exited, Dr. Cherry looked at them and said, "Where're you girls going? The boat doesn't leave until 6 o'clock."

Dickie Johnston, Back to Pass

 What do former Tennessee basketball players have good to say about Vanderbilt? Probably not much, due to the intense rivalry that has developed between the two schools through the years. The Volunteers and Commodores have had some great battles on the hardwood, and their love/hate relationship reached its peak during the Mears Era at Tennessee. Entering Memorial Coliseum in the 1970's as a Volunteer basketballer was comparable to experiencing a nightmare.

On game nights huge banners hung from the inside of their arena, and none welcomed the visitors from Knoxville. Comparing their school to Disneyland, one banner read: "Welcome to Vandyland." Bill Justus, the All American wingman for the Vols, had his own personal sign: "Bill Justus likes boys." Even the entire Volunteer community had a banner welcoming them to Memorial Coliseum: "Nothing sucks like a Big Orange." When the Vols visited Nashville, Vanderbilt seemed to always put their worst foot forward.

In 1971 oranges rained from the stands and, unfortunately, started a bad fad at other SEC schools when the Vol teams came to compete. With under a minute left to play Volunteer point guard Dickie Johnston while dribbling the ball approached mid-court. The Vols, with a substantial lead, were waiting for the final seconds to tick off and then a pleasant plane trip back to Knoxville.

However, just as Dickie crossed the center stripe, the unthinkable happened: An orange sailed out of the student section and struck Dickie directly in the side of the head. He pulled up his dribble, put the ball under his arm, and just stood there like he was in deep thought. He appeared stunned by the blow. Next, unthinkable number two happened: Dickie took the ball and threw it into the Vanderbilt student section. Not believing his eyes, a team-mate mumbled: "Dickie, you didn't do that, did you?" In a second it was obvious he had, as dozens and dozens of oranges were discharged onto the court. Everyone was looking for a foxhole but direct hits were everywhere. No one could get it stopped. Coach Mears and Coach Aberdeen became targets. If you were in orange, you were in trouble. Players streaked to the locker room faster than a pre-season drill. The entire field house smelled like a Sunkist orange juice factory. Peelings, pulp and juice were everywhere. The locker room served as a battle bunker, a safe haven, so to speak.

On the plane, several people asked John Ward, "The Voice of the Vols," what his call was on the radio regarding the incident. John did the replay on the plane: "Dickie Johnston brings the ball across half court, pulls up, drops back and throws a long pass downfield complete to the Vanderbilt student body. Give him six. Touchdown Tennessee!"

No doubt many Vols who peel an orange over the Christmas holidays are reminded of the night it rained oranges in a college field house.

The Vanderbilt Game Plan

When the Vols played in Nashville against Vanderbilt, Coach Ray Mears had a custom of taking a long, slow walk around the court of Memorial Coliseum preceding the game. Accompanying him for the walk was his bodyguard Olympic javelin thrower and UT track athlete Bill Skinner. During Coach Mears' jaunt the entire arena would erupt in a chorus of boos with a little profanity mingled in. There was never any love lost when Tennessee met Vandy in Nashville. Traditionally each year Mears would make the hike, the fans would boo, and then the Commodores would usually lose.

After several years of disappointment, the Nashville sportswriters finally solved the mystery: They wrote articles stating that Mears was psyching everyone out, including the Vandy Team, when he took the pre-game stroll. The booing and degrading remarks were only firing up Tennessee, and this is why Vandy was losing. When Coach Mears took his next walk after the articles were published in the paper, the Vandy fans took a new approach as they stood and cheered him for what seemed like eternity. It was obvious Mears was overcome with emotion as he entered the locker room. It was the first time the team had ever seem him smile prior to a game; and, oh yes, the Commodores lost again.

Waiting on a Flight

When being recruited by a major university to play athletics, one meets some individuals who have been highly successful in their fields. During my senior year my family and I had the opportunity to talk with several of these fine people. All were naturally graduates of the university that was attempting to recruit the student athlete.

In 1969 three businessmen, two from Knoxville and one from Indianapolis, visited our home in Greenfield, Indiana, and talked with my family and me about the advantages of attending the University of Tennessee. Their very professional and businesslike presentation informed us of the tremendous job Coach Mears had done with the basketball program and how the arena was sold out for all the games. One gentleman remarked: "Coach Mears is putting the school on the basketball map." Boasting of the institution's academic records and the good education one could obtain on "the hill," they related that many UT graduates entered the corporate world and had become very successful. The diplomatic representatives emphasized the friendliness of the UT campus and portrayed the natural beauty of the area lakes and mountains. Other promotions were the outstanding athletic facilities and the fact the university ran a first-class program.

Being interested in playing for the Vols, I was very impressed with their presentation which gave me a little different perspective of what the school had to offer and the benefits after graduation. The Hoosier businessman appeared to me to be a genuine person who manifested integrity.

After all the discussions on the University, the recruiters queried my parents regarding any concerns. Their response, which was the same one they made to any coaches from schools further than 90 miles from Greenfield, Indiana, was: "We have followed Mike all through high school and we're concerned that if he leaves the state we won't get to see him play." This matter, usually met with silence if the school was a long distance from Greenfield, was supposedly solved by Assistant Coach at UCLA Denny Crum when he stated:

"You are only three hours from Los Angeles by plane." Well, it might be three hours by plane to Los Angeles, but my folks had three other sons to support and paying to take a plane to LA was just not going to happen.

One of the gentleman from Tennessee had the perfect solution by stating: "It's only six hours from Greenfield so you could leave Greenfield in the morning and make it in plenty of time to see Mike play on Saturday nights." Then the successful Indianapolis representative made a suggestion that my family has sarcastically enjoyed over the past thirty years. He said their corporate plane would be available to fly Mom and Dad to Knoxville for some of the games.

Well, all during my playing career my parents waited on the flight. The Alabama games passed, the Kentucky games passed, and the LSU games passed. Very soon the four years passed but still no promised flight. On the contrary, Mom and Dad wore out enough tires on their car to last a lifetime. Dad drove so may trips to Knoxville he said he just left the driveway and closed his eyes and let the car drive them automatically to the city on the river.

For the next thirty years when I called my parents and asked them if they were coming down to Maryville to visit, Dad's sarcastic response usually was, "Taking the corporate plane, we'll be down in a couple of hours; can you pick us up at the airport?" Well, Dad passed away a couple years ago, but Mom is still waiting on the flight.

Cab Deal

During our SEC championship year in 1971-72, we had a point guard named Steve Hirschorn. Steve was small in size but big in heart. He moved into the starting point guard position midway through the year and provided the leadership we needed in our run to the top.

Steve was the best businessman I ever met, at least while I was in college. Always looking for a deal, he obviously made a lot of good decisions because he always dressed nice and seemed to have money to do a lot of extra activities.

While we were in New York for the Holiday Festival Basketball Tournament, I found out the hard way why Steve always had money. We were in the lobby of the City Squire Hotel waiting for taxis to take us to a local gym to practice. Bud Ford, our sports information director, had five cabs lined up in front of the building and told all the players and coaches to divide into five groups, one group for each cab. Bud then handed one player from each group twenty dollars for the cab fare. Hirschorn was one of the five given money. We all headed for the cabs and were on our way to practice. Upon arriving at our destination, the driver requested the fare. All those in our group looked at each other like homeless people without a nickel. No one in our cab had any money.

Hirschorn saw a possible money making opportunity. Seeing four other players get twenty dollars, Steve took his twenty and boarded one of their cabs. That left one taxi minus a fare and that happened to be ours. That was one disturbed driver and I have always heard you should not upset New York cabbies; however, all of us exited the vehicle and headed for the gym as if the city of New York was obligated to pick up the tab, leaving Lloyd Richardson behind to explain. We figured Lloyd could solve the dilemma since he was the captain of the team.

It was after this incident that I realized Steve Hirschorn was the master magician when it came to money. No doubt, he was headed for a great career in business.

Winning Your Heart

After a hard-fought game in Tuscaloosa against Alabama on a Saturday afternoon, Coach Mears flew us to Baton Rouge, Louisiana, to prepare for the LSU Tigers. The Tigers were playing the league-leading Kentucky Wildcats that night, and Coach wanted us to attend the game to observe the Tiger personnel. Dale Brown was in his first year as the LSU coach, and he was desperately trying to promote his program to the fans that had lost some interest after the departure of Pete Maravich.

On this night Brown had tried to promote the game as if it were something out of a John Wayne western. Ushers passed out flyers to the fans on which in bold letters at the top was the word "Wanted." Below this word appeared a team picture of the Kentucky squad (the bad guys), and just below the Kentucky picture were some of Coach Brown's players dressed in cowboy attire (the good guys). Below the portrait of the LSU players the flyer read, "These guys will win your hearts."

As we took our seats I noticed two LSU fans directly in front of us, looking at the poster. Then one of them turned to the other and said, "This team might win my heart but they're going to lose their ass tonight." They did; Kentucky beat the living tar out of them.

Wrap It in Orange

Coach Mears always believed that the week before the LSU game the Tigers and their coach Dale Brown would spend all their practice time preparing for Tennessee. They were scheduled to play Kentucky before our encounter on Monday, but one could easily conclude by the lopsided thrashing they received by the Cats on Saturday their coaching staff was not convinced they could win. However, when Monday rolled around, LSU was a different team altogether against the Vols. In fact, it is believed that LSU kept us from winning the SEC championship three consecutive years because we split the series with them and that one game cost us at the end.

In 1973 we were in Baton Rouge to face the Tigers in a must-win situation. If we lost, we were probably out of the SEC chase because we had lost to Alabama on the previous Saturday, and a road trip with two losses would be devastating. John Ward, the voice of the Vols, called some great basketball games. He was so outstanding that several people in my hometown of Greenfield, Indiana, taped the games and still cherish the tapes today. One of his great calls came in the LSU game in 1973.

With five seconds to go and the game tied, the Volunteers had the ball ninety-four feet from their basket, and Coach Mears signaled a time out. To this day I do not know how in the world we got a shot off. Here's the call by Ward: "Robinson inbounds the ball to Rodney Woods who streaks to half court on the dribble and lifts a long pass to the cutting Edwards in the corner who fires a twenty-five footer." There is silence on the radio; then the voice erupts: "Wrap it in orange!"

Let the Big Dog Sleep

 In 1994 I invited Coach Mears to participate in my placement on the Indiana Silver Anniversary Team at the Hall of Fame Banquet. It was a great trip to Hoosierland, and I enjoyed visiting with Coach Mears on the way up, rehashing the past and talking basketball. We planned to stay at my parents' house in Greenfield. It just so happened that Purdue was playing in the NCAA Tournament, and Mears had an added interest in that game. Al Brown, an assistant coach for the Lady Vols at the time, had told him he could obtain tickets for the next round if Purdue won.

While watching the Purdue game on television from my parents' home, we had no doubt whom Coach favored. He had been transformed into a Boilermaker fan. Glen Robinson, nicknamed "Big Dog," was Purdue's main man. Well, "Big Dog" or whatever, I can tell you that my parents were Indiana Bob Knight fans; and regardless of whomever Purdue was playing, Mom and Dad would pull for their opponents. I do not know why Dad disliked Purdue so much, but I think it was because he worked with a lot of PHD graduates of Purdue who claimed they knew as much about sports as they did about antibiotics. Dad never graduated from college, but he was an excellent lab worker for Lilly's, and he enjoyed putting the college boys "in their place." He even had a name for the Purdue PHD's—"Poor Helpless Devils."

During the game, Coach Mears kept talking about "Big Dog"—"Big Dog" this and "Big Dog" that. It looked like the Boilers were going to pull the contest out. "Nice play by the Purdue guard" and "boy, 'Big Dog' can jump; what a great pro prospect," Coach remarked. Dad kept watching and listening to Coach Mears but remained silent. You could surely read what was going through his mind: "I hope they get their ass beat; they just play alley ball."

In the last minute Purdue lost a heart breaker. Dad immediately arose from his chair and walked directly to the TV, turning it off. With apparent satisfaction, he said, "We'll let the 'Big Dog' sleep now."

Anywhere But Kentucky

In the spring of 1973 I interviewed at New Castle High School in Indiana for their vacant head basketball position. New Castle was one of the premier coaching slots in the state. The school boasted the largest high school gymnasium in the world, seating over 10,000. The players who came from the school were legendary in the high school and college basketball ranks—Ray Pavy, Kent Benson, and Steve Alford, to name a few.

During my interview at New Castle, a couple of unique propositions were presented: First, while discussing the prerequisites for the job, I asked the athletic director what subjects I would be required to teach. He said: "You can have six study halls if you want them; we are hiring you to run the basketball program from grade school through high school and to win games." During my entire coaching career on the high school and college level, never have I experienced a program like that; I was always required to teach at least three academic classes.

Secondly, also during the interview Coach Mears became part of the discussion. He had recruited New Castle star Kent Benson through his high school years, making several trips to see him perform. Coach Mears thought he had a good chance of influencing Kent to come to Knoxville; however, a few weeks before my interview, Kent informed Coach Mears he was no longer interested in the Vols. Of course, Coach Mears was disappointed because Benson was one of the outstanding big men in the United States.

But Mears' problem with losing Benson went deeper than losing an outstanding recruit. Kentucky was still on the star center's list and if coach could not have him on his team, he was going to make sure he did not have to play against him. So Mears continued to recruit Benson, encouraging him to stay in the state of Indiana where his fans from New Castle could see him play. "Indiana boys should remain at home," Coach emphasized, while continuing to call Kent and even making a trip or two to pitch the stay-at-home approach. Kent must have heeded the advice because he signed with Indiana University and played a vital part in assisting the Hoosiers in winning a national championship. No doubt Bob Knight appreciated all of coach's efforts, and "The General" should have felt obligated to present Coach Mears a championship ring.

That incident is the first I have ever heard of a major college coach expending recruiting time to encourage a player to attend a school against which the coach would not have to compete. Coach Mears had one goal when he lost Kent Benson—"Anywhere but Kentucky."

Down for the Count

During the Ron Widby era the Volunteers were preparing to play Auburn and then Kentucky; it was traditionally one of the most difficult weeks of practice during the season. The players could expect a lot of physical activity in the workouts because that was the way the Tigers always performed against them. Auburn played an aggressive man-to-man defense and was known for a few cheap-shot elbows during the contest.

Before each practice during the week, Coach Aberdeen pulled Mike Humphries, a second-team player, to the side and talked to him about assisting the Vols in practice by playing aggressively during the scrimmage. Coach had Humphries so motivated that he felt like a win or loss depended on his performance in practice. Instructing Mike that he would be guarding Ron Widby, Aberdeen encouraged Mike to push, elbow, and mouth Ron every chance he got which would improve Widby's mental toughness.

Well, Humphries did not disappoint Aberdeen; he threw some elbows at Ron, pushed him around, and mouthed him constantly. Widby asked him politely to stop, but Humphries continued to follow his coach's directions and just laughed at him while taunting him again. Finally, Ron, having his fill, turned and looked at Humphries and said, "If you push or elbow me one more time, I'm going to beat the living shit out of you."

On the next play Humphries put a direct elbow into the All American's chest and what followed was ugly. Widby reared back and hit Humphries with an upper right, sailing him across the floor like Superman. He landed in the chairs on the side court with his eyes rolled back, lip cut and a few teeth loosened. He looked like he had been involved in an automobile wreck before the rescue unit had arrived.

With Humphries in desperate need of medical attention, the coaching staff ran directly to Widby. Coach Mears, his eyes revealing concern said, "Ron, is your hand all right? You know you shouldn't have done that; if you break that hand, you could be out for the season. Let me take a look at it." Widby was getting firsthand treatment while Humphries was bleeding profusely and gasping for air.

The Vols won the game against Auburn and Mike Humphries survived to practice another day. He probably defended more than the right to practice but such was the life for a second team player whose job week in and week out in the Mears' system was to get the varsity ready to play.

Eating Soap

I told you earlier about one of the Tennessee players, Steve Hirschorn, being small in stature and big in heart. He was all that and more because during his underclassman days he got picked on a lot by the older players, especially when he was a freshman and sophomore. It might have been because of his size or it could have been because "Hirsch" had a tendency to be opinionated. Regardless, he had a way of upsetting some of the veteran players. One such player was noted to be the meanest Vol to ever wear the orange and white and answered to no one.

The bullying Vol felt that all freshmen should grow up fast and that they needed a little more discipline than Coach Mears was applying. So every night during their study session in the dorm he would round them up—Hirschorn included, march them into the bathroom, and hand them a small unopened bar of soap. He then told them to open the soap and eat it.

Now the aggressive prankster was a big guy, and there was not one freshman that could handle him. So the soap was eaten by all gladly. This soap eating got to be such a nightly ritual that when the overbearing upperclassman came into Hirschorn's room, Hirsch made sure he had his own supply at his desk and he would simply take out a bar and begin eating it right there. Can you imagine a choice of eating soap or getting the crap beat out of you? Such was a part of the initiation ordeals of a Tennessee basketball freshman.

Running Bare

One cold January night the veteran players got tired of making the freshmen eat soap, so they decided to pull another stunt. It was fifteen degrees above zero outside, and the wind was howling. To be honest, it was damn cold.

The veteran players looked up and down the dormitory hall for a freshman, but none could be found. Hearing the water running in the shower, they decided to check who was in there. Unfortunately for the freshman who was showering, the night was about to get colder. Taking the poor guy out of the shower and down the hall clad in only "his birthday suit," they put him in a car. Soaking wet, the underclassman was driven to the Presidential Complex on campus where stood four of the tallest student dorms. After driving him to the center of the complex with students walking all around, the veteran players let him loose.

This escapade might have been the first streaking incident on the UT campus because that fad did not start until years later. The young Vol made it back to the athletic dorm with frozen hair and blue lips, setting a record by being the fastest naked runner on the Tom Black Track, which he had to cross to get back to the dorm.

Where Death Doesn't Stop Basketball

A few years ago while on a trip to my hometown of Greenfield, Indiana, I pulled my car up to a traffic light on Main Street and looked to my right. Just before the light changed, an ambulance from Pasco's Mortuary drove up next to me. Dave Pasco was driving. I waved and rolled my window down to greet him. The first words out of his mouth were: "Did you play in the NCAA Tournament or the NIT?"

I couldn't believe it; after all these years having seen Dave a very few times, I was asked a basketball question on the main street of town. It was great—just like old times! This man was transporting a dead body to the funeral home in the middle of summer and he had Tennessee basketball on his mind. It proved to me the more things change in Indiana, the more they remain the same, especially when it comes to basketball.

Poet or Cat?

At a pre-season basketball banquet during my freshman year, Coach Mears introduced me to the crowd as follows: "Next is Mike Edwards, from Greenfield, Indiana. Greenfield is the home of James Whitcomb Riley." Just as Coach finished saying "Riley," a southern gentleman arose from the back of the room and blurted out: "Riley—wasn't he a great guard at Kentucky?"

Sorry, wrong Riley. This one was a poet. But Pat Riley was an outstanding player at Kentucky. I have never researched him, but maybe he was related to Jim. The poet Riley was famous for writing the poems: *Little Orphant Annie, When the Frost Is on the Pumpkin,* and *The Raggedy Man,* among others.

Tiger Bait

When we played LSU in their beautiful arena, which was built with the money and enthusiasm from the Pete Maravich years, one fan always seemed to make his presence apparent. This Tiger fan sat at the very top of the arena. He was, without a doubt, one of their most ardent fans; but he had been given one of the worst seats in the house. Perhaps he could never donate enough money to the school to qualify for a better seat. Nonetheless, this fan always made his presence known.

As the opposing team came onto the court, this devoted fan stood and chanted: "Tiger bait! Tiger bait! Tiger bait!" Starting slowly and softly, he proceeded to get faster and louder with the chant until he involved the entire arena. This guy had the loudest voice and the biggest mouth I have every heard at a sporting event. He caused the entire arena to vibrate without even a microphone. Chanting only during the pre-game ceremony, perhaps he over-extended himself so much during that period that he was unable to yell during the game.

Subsequent to Tennessee's games at Baton Rouge, which netted us wins three consecutive years, Len Kosmalski enjoyed mimicking this Tiger fanatic. Upon boarding the team bus after the games, Len would begin imitating the LSU sideshow actor by chanting, "Tiger bait! Tiger bait! Tiger bait!"

The Southern Gentleman

There are two prominent recollections of my recruiting visit to the University of Tennessee in the spring of 1969: First, I had already toured the campus in the previous fall, so I asked Coach Mears if I could go fishing when I came south for my final visit. Perhaps this was the first time any recruit had made a request of this nature.

Feeling a little helpless with this appeal, Coach Mears assigned Jimmy England to assume the recruiting task on the lake. We did not catch many fish that day, but I learned from Jimmy all the spots that did not contain fish. Therefore, when I came to the university I made sure I did not waste any time fishing there again. I also learned from Jim how slowly southerners talk. It took so long for him to complete a sentence that by the time he finished I had forgotten what his initial words were. Anyway, I had a great time on the lake that day and learned a lot about the UT program from Jim.

My other memorable experience occurred when Coach Mears drove me to the home of UT President Andy Holt for a visit. Situated on the Tennessee River, the stately house was located in a beautiful section of Knoxville. President Holt was one of the most personable individuals I had ever met, and epitomized the southern gentleman. Contributing to the comfort of a young lad who was 360 miles from home, he manifested warmth and kindness.

We discussed briefly Tennessee basketball and the University, but the majority of our conversation involved fishing. I realized that when you mention fishing to Dr. Holt, all the shoptalk came to a halt. It was the only time in my recruiting process that Coach Mears remained totally silent. It was evident that "wetting a line" held little interest for him.

I enjoyed that short meeting with President Holt, and all during my career at the University of Tennessee he never forgot me. Attending almost every home basketball game, he always sat directly behind the goal; so when warming up, I always looked for him. On occasion he would send me a note of congratulations on an athletic or academic achievement. He was certainly a president who had earned the love and respect of all the students.

The following is a letter from Dr. Holt that I received at the end of my junior year:

May 2, 1972

Dear Mike,

Congratulations on your selection as a member of the Academic All-American Third Team! I do not see how under the sun you are able to find time to maintain such an excellent academic record and still spend as much time as you do practicing for basketball.

We are extremely proud to have you as a student at UT!

Please let me know when and if you find time for a bit of fishing this spring or summer.

Sincerely,

Andy Holt

Dr. Holt touched a lot of students' lives and wrote several letters encouraging them to excel. He made every student feel important with his infectious smile and a pat on the back. They do not make many Andy Holts any more; he was one of a kind—a true southern gentleman. I'm so glad our paths crossed.

Roll Out the Carpet for . . .

When Coach Mears recruited players, he used a unique approach. The recruiting process was accomplished with all the flamboyance and flare of his pre-game warm-up drills. When he came to observe your performance in high school games, he wore his orange blazer. He stood out in the crowd like the sun on a cloudy day. The lighting in the gym enhanced the blazer's brightness.

When it came to recruiting, Mears displayed expertise. He will tell you that when he recruited a player, he recruited the mother just as intensely. His belief was that if you sold the mother, you would sell her son. While I was being recruited I can personally attest to this process. Phone calls were made and cards were sent to my Mom. He even discovered she was originally from Rock Island, Tennessee, with relatives residing in Byrdstown, Tennessee. (After a few months of these enforcement tactics by Mears, I jestingly asked my Mom what position she intended to play and informed her that the practices were going to be extremely demanding.) Coach Mears was successful in using these methods to recruit young lads. Several players signed package deals at universities at that time that demanded the hiring of their high school coach also. During the Mears era, the package was mother and son.

Mears recruited one of the best big men out of the eastern part of the United States. His name was Tommy Roy. Of course, the Vol mentor was not the only coach interested in Roy; every coach in the nation coveted him. He was a household name to basketball experts. The school that signed him would be guaranteed success.

When Mears scheduled Roy's recruiting visit to Knoxville, he decided to put on a show. Coach made him believe that everybody in Tennessee wanted him to play for the Vols. He lined up the flight to Knoxville, making certain the cheerleaders; pep band; all the coaching staff; and a few orange tie boosters were present when Roy alighted. And, oh yes, he demanded an orange carpet be rolled out to welcome the prize recruit. However, there was one potential problem that coach had not anticipated.

Bob Knight, who at that time was head coach at Army, was scheduled to be the guest speaker at UT's basketball clinic that same weekend. Well, the West Point mentor was a step ahead of Coach Mears. Knight wanted Roy in his program. So he found out through Roy which flight he was scheduled to arrive in Knoxville, and Knight purchased his ticket for the same flight. When Tommy stepped off the plane, the cheerleaders went into their routine and the pep band played the school fight song as Mears and other dignitaries stood at the front of the orange-carpeted tarmac, awaiting Roy. As the high school All-American stepped off the plane and approached Coach Mears, Bob Knight suddenly rushed past the prized recruit and confronted Mears. Knight looked at the bewildered Mears and said, "Hell, Coach, you didn't have to do all this for me!"

Well, neither Mears nor Knight succeeded in obtaining Tommy Roy; he signed with another great "showman" and recruiter, Lefty Dreisell of Maryland.

Playing Vandy?—Just Send a Substitute

I had an economics teacher at UT who was adamantly strict regarding class attendance. As part of her first day procedures, she announced there would be no make-ups; being absent for a test or quiz regardless of the reason was not an option. Since the Vols' SEC away games were scheduled on Saturdays and Mondays, team members always missed those Monday classes.

During the Vandy-Auburn swing this teacher scheduled a test for a Monday. On the Friday prior to the road game, I informed her that I was a member of the basketball team and that I could not take the test on Monday due to the basketball trip. I requested the possibility of rescheduling the test for Tuesday, emphasizing that some Mondays we would be out of town and that attending class was impossible during those times. The professor's unforgettable remarks were: "I do not give make-ups; if you are not here, the test will be scored a zero. You need to tell the coach to send a back-up player for you if you want to get credit for the exam."

Confronted with a dilemma, I had two choices: Ask Coach Mears if I could remain home and send a substitute for me or go to the drop and add window, eliminating this class and teacher forever. Approaching Coach Mears was not a rational alternative; that would have been similar to going to a shark tank with a huge piece of bloody meat in my mouth and jumping in. So I went to the drop window and kissed that teacher's class good-bye.

A Great One Attends

For the Vols' opening game in the 1971-72 season Coach Mears invited one of the greatest basketball coaches that ever lived to attend. Ray Mears of Tennessee and Bob Knight of Texas Tech were two coaches that this individual's basketball philosophy influenced as they implemented his highly disciplined approach, his defenses, and his various offensive sets. Coach Knight, while coaching at Army, met with this coach extensively, and Mears spent a year with him learning his system. Press Maravich, the coach at LSU during the Mears era at Tennessee, was an excellent player for this basketball legend.

Most current fans were unaware of the notoriety this marvelous coach had attained in the 1930's There are probably only a few people today that remember him attending the season opener in 1971 because through the years little has been written regarding his presence at that game.

This coach won 357 games and lost only 79 with a winning percentage of .819. Coaching eighteen seasons at Long Island University, his teams at one point compiled a forty-three consecutive-game winning streak. He coached LIU to two undefeated seasons (1935-36 and 1938-39), and his teams won two NIT championships. In a thirteen-year span his LIU teams compiled an astonishing 222-3 home record. He developed the 1-3-1-zone defense and was influential in the three-second rule. The "great one" who was present for the Vols' home opener in 1971 was Clair Bee, one of the game's most spectacular coaches and a member of the National Basketball Hall of Fame.

Ball Four

We were in the locker room getting ready to play archrival Vanderbilt, and Coach Mears had just finished a fiery motivational speech. Upon completing his vehement rhetoric, he pulled an orange from his blazer pocket, placed it in his left hand, and remarked, "Remember what Vandy does to you when we go to Nashville?" He then wound up and threw the orange with all the velocity of a Nolan Ryan. The orange hit the front wall and exploded like a grenade, spraying several players with its remnants. The players then ran out of the locker room, giving each other high fives and headed for the arena floor.

Five minutes into the warm-up all the Volunteer team was accounted for but one: Coach Mears had not made his appearance on the floor. Now this was a first because Coach was always on the floor to watch us warm up. He thought the tempo for the game was set during the warm-up session and any mistakes in the fancy ball handling routines would mean we were not mentally prepared to play. We all waited for Coach to arrive, thinking he had some new gimmick for the Commodores up his sleeve—maybe some grand entrance to distract them.

Having concluded our pre-game warm up and heading back to the locker room for final instructions, we learned the fate of Coach Mears. He was talking to the athletic trainer and appeared to be in quite a bit of pain. The orange toss proved to be costly motivation; Coach had thrown his shoulder out of socket with his left-handed pitch.

When the players discovered what had occurred, the incident seemed to result in ridding them of the pre-game tension; and, consequently, we played one of our best games of the season. In this case only the result of the motivational speech made the difference, instead of the talk itself. Coach spent the entire evening moving his left shoulder up and down, trying to pop it back in place.

By the way, Coach's fast pitch would have been labeled a ball; it was high and way outside when it hit the front meeting room wall.

Who's the Leading Scorer?

During the pre-game warm up, the "White Trash Team" (second team) had a special routine. When the players who would start were shooting in preparation for the game, the "trash," knowing they probably were not going to play, decided to have their own game. Subsequent to the Globetrotters' warm-up drills Coach Mears paired two players to a basketball to work on their shooting. Most athletes worked at their own individual pace during the shooting session, but some of us noticed several of the players, noticeably Roger Peltz, shooting and then moving to get the ball and then shooting again. They put on an awesome display of speed shooting. Most of us did not know what was going on. We assumed they were attempting to impress somebody; we just did not know whom.

When we returned to the locker room for final instructions, we found out what was occurring. The "trash team's" goal was to see who could score the most points with all shots being taken at least fifteen feet out. At the end of the warm up they would sit down in the meeting room and ask each other: "How many points did you score?" Sometimes they accused one another of not being truthful, using a few salty words. At times the competition got very intense. If the coaches had been aware of their scheme, they could have presented an award for the most points scored in pre-game warm-ups at the year-end banquet.

Tennessee—I Have a Problem

Every fall the time would arrive for that dreaded athletic requirement—the yearly physical. To find out if we were physically qualified to participate, each athlete was required to go to the UT Medical Center on campus to be pecked on, probed and violated. Wires were hooked up to us to see if the heart was functioning properly; eyes and ears were checked; and knees were examined. Upon completion of the thorough check-up, one would have thought he had endured an examination that qualified him for a moon trip.

One year I decided to experiment with some pills my Mother had given me. Supposedly they would turn one's urine different colors. Unaware of how Mom obtained them, I was assured they were safe. (My Mom worked in a doctor's office.) A couple of guys were big on protein supplements that built muscles at the time, so I decided to see if the pills worked. I gave one of the players two of the pills the morning of the physical exams and told him they were a new supplement guaranteeing muscle buildup. College guys will try anything, so the player downed these two pills without hesitation.

When we reported for our physicals later that morning, this athlete was presented with a urine specimen-sample cup. Remaining in the restroom a little longer than usual, he finally appeared exhibiting the countenance of a dead man. He handed the nurse the most beautiful Tennessee-orange urine you could ever imagine. A shade all of its own, it was really more vivid than the true Tennessee color. Approaching the nurse, he said: "Ma'am, I have a problem."

Thrown to the Wolf

Tennessee basketball practices were tough! A typical day consisted of rising early, eating breakfast and then attending class from 8 a.m. until 1:50 p.m. At 2:30 p.m. we reported to the basketball meeting room for thirty minutes of motivation. The meeting could be positive; but if the team was not playing well or Coach was not in the best of moods, it could be a long session.

Each player sat in chairs according to his rank on the team, the goal being to sit in one of the first five chairs. The captain always qualified for a white chair, but everyone else had an orange chair. One might wonder what a coach would have to say for thirty minutes every day; but Coach Mears was a master at speaking, and I assure you he was unmindful of the clock during these sessions. He had a real knack at criticizing a player for the entire time period without ever mentioning his name; however, everyone in the room knew exactly to whom he was referring.

Even though we were required to be prompt, at times it was impossible, especially if you failed to follow the staff's highly disciplined requirements. One day I was running late due to a test I had just finished. When I arrived at my locker, the laces on my basketball shoes had been removed and were tied in knots. The shoes were in a mess with the laces so tangled it would have been simpler to have gone to the Cumberland Strip and purchased some new shoes. A note beside the entangled mess read: "I did this—Coach Aberdeen. Next time unlace the shoes properly."

This meeting was just the beginning of a long day. After the session, Coach Mears worked on offense for two and one-half hours. He took pride in telling recruits that he spent three-fourths of his practice time on offense because opposing coaches would tell recruits that Tennessee was a defensive school. While Coach Aberdeen was at the opposite end of the court working the living tar out of the team's big men, Mears would have the guards and forwards shooting the basketball.

This shooting session lasted one hour. Coach worked with me individually, encouraging me to shoot the ball from farther and farther out. He felt that the farther I could take shots from the basket, the more it opened up the inside for our center, Len Kosmalski. The most far out he let me shoot in a game was two or three feet across the half court line. If I had another year of eligibility and another year of shooting work with him, he might have let me take a shot from half court. Coach's philosophy was that if you can do it, I am going to give you the green light.

The last hour of practice was all Coach Aberdeen's time. He was in charge of the defense. At this point in the workout no one had any legs left and most had quit sweating. The glands had no perspiration left. It was during this session that one endured some of the most memorable one-liners of Vol basketball lore:

"Son, your defensive stance looks like a pregnant fox at a forest fire."

"It's a good thing you came to Tennessee; those other schools wouldn't have taken the time to red shirt you."

"Son, just keep your mouth shut and play; you sound like a turkey—gobble, gobble, gobble."

"You've been spoon-fed all your life."

"Give me cops' kids and firemen's kids; they're tough. You're just a cake eater."

"Boy, if I were playing against you, I'd just laugh at you; you are so bad today."

"You're playing so poorly today; why don't you just transfer?"

"Guys, don't worry terribly about sweating; it's not going to break your face out."

"We're going to give you 'best dressed' on campus; forget the basketball."

Coach Aberdeen was the expert at testing a player's mental toughness. If Coach were still around for today's practices, most athletes would have lawyers lined up to sue him for mental abuse or they would be begging to go to a guidance counselor to talk because their self-esteem had been destroyed.

Coach Aberdeen's methods made us all better basketball players; but beyond that, he was preparing us for challenges we would encounter later in life. Emphasizing hard work, his philosophy was: If you did not earn something, it was not worth having. We were all better prepared for bumps in the road of life after experiencing Coach Aberdeen's tactics, even though the last hour of practice was like being thrown to the wolves.

Where's Norman?

When we were on the road to play a game, Coach Mears always took us to church to worship on Sunday; and, of course, we wore our orange blazers to display the university we represented.

While in New York City to participate in a tournament, we had the opportunity to attend the church where Norman Vincent Peale served as pastor. Coach Mears was quite excited that we were having the opportunity to hear this renowned minister preach a sermon. However, when we arrived at the church, there was no room in the sanctuary. Consequently, we were escorted to an adjoining room where it was impossible to view Dr. Peale. We were able to hear him speak only. This was my first experience of attending a church without the benefit of observing the minister.

Last Will

We had just locked up an NIT bid by defeating archrival Vanderbilt, and it was decision time for somebody. Nashville was experiencing a wicked blizzard with three or four inches of snow on the ground and howling winds. The atmosphere reminded me of nor'easters we were accustomed to in Indiana. I expected to spend the night in Nashville, celebrating the victory and heading back to Knoxville the next morning.

I did not enjoy flying on a clear day, let alone in a blinding blizzard. When I entered the plane my hands were wet with perspiration. Sitting with the team chaplain to secure an extra portion of comfort, I never experienced total ease until the plane landed in Knoxville. I remember the team chaplain, Reverend James Tipton who was a former Penn State football player, attempted to calm me by saying, "Mike, don't worry; when your number's up, it's going to be up." My quick response was, "I understand, but I don't want to be on a plane when that pilot's number is up."

We were on the bus ready to leave the Nashville hotel when the shocking news came from Bud Ford, the Sports Information Director in charge of travel: "I just talked to the airport and they informed me they think they can get the plane up. The weather is okay toward Knoxville."

I could not believe it; I really did not like that word *think*. On the journey to the airport it seemed like our bus was the only vehicle moving. There were semi-trucks jackknifed and cars off the road everywhere. On arriving at the airport, our bus was driven directly to the airplane. They quickly herded us onto the plane, loading the luggage, and down the runway we went. I thought it was all over, believing it would take a miracle just to lift the plane off the ground. You could not have pried my hands with a crowbar from the back of the seat in front of me. The pilot managed to maneuver the plane into the air, but the worst was yet to come. That plane moved from side to side and up and down; at times I thought we were flying upside down. Even team members who were not intimidated by flying revealed terror in their eyes.

When that plane suddenly dropped one hundred feet, some of the supposedly brave aviators had all they could take. It was time for their Last Will to be delivered. "You can have my car," one team member said. "You can have my stereo," another echoed. "You can have what money I've got and my clothes," remarked another terrified player. All at once, as the plane dropped another one hundred feet, the ultimate final will was vocalized, "You can have my girlfriend!"

Nicknames

University of Tennessee basketball was no different from sports of another day or time in the fact that athletes were called nicknames. Sportscasters or sportswriters initiated some of these monikers but most were given to players by teammates. Some players were called by their middle names, some nicknames were a result of their appearance, and others came from their origin. Some of the nicknames would follow the player to their grave but others were gone as quickly as they were given. A few of the names caused problems for some of us.

For instance, soon after my graduation from the University I took a position with the Blount National Bank in Maryville, Tennessee. Referring to my hometown in Indiana, I had been labeled the "Greenfield Gunner" at UT by John Ward, the Voice of the Vols. At the bank one day a customer approached me and shouted, "There's the Greenfield Gunner!" Not being a UT basketball fan and unfamiliar with my nickname, the manager of the bank branch immediately pushed the alarm button. Assuming the bank was being robbed, police cars surrounded the building in a matter of minutes. The entire incident looked like a scene out of the movie *Naked Gun.*

The following are a few nicknames the Vol basketball family acquired during the Ray Mears Era. Do you recognize any?

Coach Stu Aberdeen—Beef
Coach Gerald Oliver—Ollie
David Mills (Manager)—General Mills
Marvin West (Sportswriter)—Scoop
Steve Hirschorn—Hirsch
Len Kosmalski—Kos
Jimmy England—Ez; Mr. Clutch
Eddie Voelker—Hair
Don Johnson—Johns
Jim Woodall—Goose
Roger Peltz—Rog
Mike Edwards—Greenfield Gunner
Lloyd Richardson—Rogersville Rifle

Wayne Tomlinson—Toms
A.W. Davis—Rutledge Rifle; "A"
Greg Hawkins—Hawk
Rudy Kinard—Rude
Kerry Myers—Killer
Billy Hann—Hondo
Tom Hendrix—Spook
Mac Petty—Blue Moon
Bill Justus—Horse
Wes Coffman—Bernie
Ron Widby—George
Tom Boerwinkle—Fred
Bernard King—Bernie; "B"
Ernie Grunfield—Ernie G
Johnny Darden—Dirt Dobber
Mike Disney—Walt

The Championship That Did Not Taste So Good

There are two kinds of games that you remember as a player: The close games you win and the close games you lose. For some reason their memory remains with you for the rest of your life. Some times you experience flashbacks, waking up in the middle of the night thinking about them. Unfortunately, if it was a loss the result is still the same in the dream.

The game that haunts me most often is the final game of the 1972 season against Kentucky. The game was major, deciding if our team would be the sole SEC Champion or share the crown with Kentucky. Coach Aberdeen told us a tie would be like "kissing your sister." The contest also decided who qualified to go to the NCAA Tournament; this was where the pressure was intense. If Kentucky won, even though there was a tie for the championship, they would get the bid because they had beaten us by two points in Lexington earlier in the season.

Much has been written about this game over the years and some of it is inaccurate. Usually rehashing the game occurs when Kentucky and Tennessee are playing in a key game and sportswriters want to emphasize the intense rivalry.

Ben Byrd, a sportswriter for *The Knoxville Journal* and an author of a book on the basketball Vols, called it "the championship that did not taste so good." I believe that Ben was partly correct but did not give everyone enough credit.

The 1971-72 season was probably one of Coach Mears' best coaching efforts. Only two starters remained from the previous year's NIT team—Lloyd Richardson and I. John Snow beat Lloyd out of his position at midyear. So, basically, Coach Mears had to replace his entire team to compete for the SEC Championship. Steve Hirschorn did a marvelous job leading the squad from the point guard position. Larry Robinson, a junior college transfer, and Len Kosmalski had stellar years. John Snow sparked the team with his outside shooting and played consistently all season. Eddie Voelker, Wayne Tomlinson, and Lloyd Richardson all contributed off the bench and played key roles in crucial situations.

The team was picked to finish fifth or sixth in most SEC pre-season polls but surprised everyone by going for the championship. However, the season ending loss to Kentucky resulted in a shared conference crown for the Vols—consequently, "a bitter-sweet championship."

Going down the stretch in the game for the SEC championship, Kentucky held a seven-point lead with less than two minutes to play. It did not look good for Tennessee, but the tables started to turn. I hit three consecutive twenty-five foot jumpers, and we were suddenly within one point with 30 seconds remaining. Kentucky brought the ball into their end of the court and then lost the ball. John Snow dove for the ball. He tied up Ronnie Lyons of Kentucky. At that time jump-ball situations were not alternated, and Snow and Lyons jumped at the foul line for possession. Tennessee controlled the tip and the Vol fans erupted. With fifteen seconds remaining, we had no time-outs.

Steve Hirschorn threw a pass inside to Len Kosmalski, and Kentucky deflected the ball out of bounds. An out-of-bounds play was called for Kos to attempt to get the ball inside to him for a high percentage shot, but the play broke down. Instead, the ball was in bounded to me in the corner and I was aggressively guarded with few options. Dribbling the ball into the foul lane, I went up for a shot and was fouled with six seconds remaining on the clock. Over the years this is where the story has gotten confused.

The rule at that time was to shoot a one-shot foul if a team was not in the bonus situation. Kentucky did not have enough fouls to give a one-plus-one free throw, so I was awarded the one shot. (The next year the rule was changed to help speed up the game: On all fouls committed before the bonus, the ball was taken out of bounds.)

So if I had hit the free throw I could have tied the game but could not have put our team in the lead as has been erroneously reported through the years; therefore, what might have occurred if the free-throw shot had gone in is only speculation. Could we have won in overtime? Kentucky still had six seconds, which was plenty of time to take a shot. Would we have fouled them, putting them on the free throw line? Would we have stolen the in-bound pass? There were a multitude of possibilities. Coach Mears claimed it should have been a two-shot foul. He said I appeared upset when I was only allowed one shot when handed the ball. He even was quoted as saying the officials made a gutless call and they were afraid of Rupp and Kentucky.

I never agreed with Coach's remarks regarding this incident because I shot eighty-six percent from the free throw line that year and have always believed that miss was one of those occurrences in a pressure situation that just did not pan out. The sports world is full of stories that have broken players' and coaches' hearts, but that is part of the game. I felt very badly for my teammates and family for a long time. Even though I have moved on with my life, there are still sportswriters and fans that were there that night that recall those last six seconds.

My Dad passed away a few years ago and I lost my best friend. He was the inspiration of my life. The night I missed that free thrown he was listening to the game on a radio in the kitchen of our home in Greenfield, Indiana. When that shot bounced off the rim, my brothers said Dad laid his head on the table and cried. Indiana people love basketball; the game is a passion with them. Dad was like a lot of Hoosiers; when your team lost, it hurt.

As low as I felt after that game, there were some incidents that occurred which convinced me the University of Tennessee was a special place. The next day after the rivalry I was scheduled to take a chemistry exam. Several of the professors offered to allow me to take the exam later if I wished. I thanked them but took the test anyway, realizing there were probably other students in the lecture hall who had problems too who were not exempt from taking the test as scheduled. I really appreciated their concern.

For several weeks I received letters from all over the state of Tennessee extending me their best wishes. I have still got most of the letters in a folder stashed away. When people through the years ask me if I made the right choice to come to Tennessee, I always remind them of the letters I received after probably one of the toughest losses that a Coach Mears team ever sustained. Tennesseans are wonderful people!

Yes, Ben Byrd, it was the championship that did not taste so good, and even after thirty years the bitterness remains in my mouth. Whenever I look at the banner hanging from Thompson-Boling that reads "1972 SEC Champions," I can still see those last six seconds. And when I put on my championship ring, which is not often, I can still see those last six seconds. Sometimes when I awaken from a dream involving the game I can see the last six seconds being replayed. Life has gone on for me and a lot of great things have happened but those last six seconds have never changed. They just hang around like a dark cloud.

NIT—You Can Forget Us

That season-ending loss to Kentucky for the SEC Title seemed to have ruined an outstanding year for a team that was not projected to do well in the conference. The locker room after the game was not a pleasant sight. It was like a cross between a morgue and a funeral; no jubilation or smiling faces were to be found anywhere.

When Coach Mears came into the locker room we learned what part emotion and despair played when one was under extreme pressure. I know Coach did not mean what he said, but he was disappointed like all of us and he just got it off his chest. He remarked that this was the hardest basketball team to motivate that he had every coached. He followed up by saying, "I want you to get together and vote on going to the NIT; I don't care what you decide."

It probably was not wise for us to make the decision that night because of the emotional factor; but heading back to the dorm, we voted by secret ballot. We cast our ballots and handed them to Lloyd Richardson, our captain. The result indicated the majority was in favor of going; however, Coach Mears informed the NIT we would not be coming. He got word that a few of the starters had voted negatively, and he did not want to take a divided team. Since we voted by secret ballot, I do not know how he concluded that some starters opted not to attend, but that was the rumor. Maybe if we had delayed the decision to vote until the next day when the emotion leveled we would have gone to New York.

I will admit that I was one who voted negatively because the NIT was a second-place tournament, and this basketball team finally tied for first. The NCAA kept a lot of great teams out of the tournament back then. Southern Cal with Paul Westphall only lost two games the entire season and stayed home because both losses were to UCLA. I felt badly for the seniors on the team, especially for Steve Hirschorn from the New York area who wanted to play in Madison Square Garden. I think it was difficult decisions like ours that opened up participation for more teams in the NCAA Tournament in the future. Whatever the consequences, the fact we had three outstanding teams but never made it to the "Big Show" remains.

It Only Takes Two to Win

Bill Justus, the Vol All-American wingman, having completed two outstanding individual scoring efforts against Georgia and Kentucky, scored thirty-five and twenty-five points respectively. The opponent Bill and his teammates faced in the next game was the Florida Gators, led by All-American center Neal Walk and coached by former Vol Assistant Coach Tommy Bartlett. Aware of Bill's success in the prior two games, the Gators concluded that restraining the All American would result in stopping the Vols.

Bill was on an offensive roll, and the entire team and staff were never more ready to play. However, Florida outfoxed them somewhat, deciding to play Tennessee a box-and-one zone with a chaser guarding Justus man-for-man. The Florida defensive scheme worked so effectively that Bill, not only scoreless, could not even get the ball. As time ran out on the clock with Florida leading by one point, Justus eluded the defense for one of the few times in the game. Launching one of his patented jump shots, he drew nothing but net.

The Vols had won a highly coveted game! Justus was carried from the floor by his teammates, one of the loftiest tributes to be bestowed on an athlete. Only attempting two shots during the entire forty minutes of play, Bill Justus hit the crucial shot that doomed the Gators and created a memory to last a lifetime! If Bill had any concern regarding his overall play for the night, he could take comfort in the fact he hit the winning shot, while shooting fifty percent for the entire evening.

The Florida coaching staff was livid, arguing that Justus had traveled prior to the shot. However, the evidence was inconclusive from the Vol coaching staff. You know how blurred those old 8 mm films could be, especially if the projector they were being run on had "Tennessee Volunteers" stamped on the side.

Who Is Having All the Fun?

The 1967 Tennessee Volunteers had just wrapped up the Southeastern Conference Championship by defeating the Mississippi State Bulldogs in a game that endured three overtimes. The contest was played in Starkville, which made the win even sweeter. With great jubilation progressing on the floor and in the locker room, the entire Volunteer basketball family were anxiously anticipating returning to Knoxville that night and engaging in some lively celebration with the student body on the Cumberland Strip; they could not wait to return to participate in one of the highlights in the Ray Mears Era.

However, just as the celebration in the locker room was subsiding, the Vol staff were handed bad news: Inclement weather had resulted in the scheduled flight to Knoxville being canceled. Highly disappointed, the team headed back to the motel and made the most of a night that had crowned them SEC Champions and presented the Vols a berth in the NCAA Tournament. The evening was spent telling jokes and playing poker.

The failure to arrive in Knoxville that night may not have been the squad's major disappointment, however; for when they finally returned to Vol Land, the newly crowned champions discovered that part of the all-night celebration on campus included the biggest panty raid in school history!

The Rent Was Not Paid

During the early seventies, Ray Mears and his staff were hot on the trail of an outstanding player from Indiana. They made several trips to a town on the Ohio River and invited the prospect and his family down for several games. Tennessee really wanted to sign this player who was later named Mr. Basketball in Indiana.

In an attempt to win the prize recruit, Tennessee utilized a unique approach: The recruit had a brother who was a year or so older than he and who was, at best, an average basketball player. The Tennessee staff offered the older brother partial financial aid, living accommodations in the athletic dormitory, and the opportunity to play on the freshmen team.

Now most of us players are not rocket scientists; however, we could see that with the basketball ability this player exhibited, he was not going to take us to a SEC championship. He was a nice guy but perhaps he would have fit in more at one of the fraternity houses than in the basketball program. This Hoosier enjoyed a good time, but I can assure you Coach Mears' program was not a trip to Disneyland. Obviously he was on the freshmen squad in hopes Tennessee could obtain his brother.

Well, the worst thing that could have happened to the poor kid occurred. His older brother committed the unforgivable—signing with the Kentucky Wildcats. The day the younger brother pledged to the Cats, the older sibling became homeless. He exited the UT athletic dorm quicker than any Volunteer in history and the assumption is that he escaped across the Kentucky line.

They Are Spying on Us

Coach Mears had a couple of favorite theories that he utilized in his pre-game and pre-practice sessions. One was the belief that everyone was "out to get him." Beating Tennessee would just about "make the other teams' year," according to Coach. Stressing that the Vols had to play errorless ball, he hypothesized the opposing team's head coaching job was on the ropes, and if they beat the Vols he would not get fired.

It seemed like every team we played except Kentucky had a coach who was on the verge of losing his position. "That coach is fighting for his life; have you ever fought for your life? These guys have their whole livelihood on the line; their house, cars, boats—they could lose it all if we beat them tonight," Mears would speculate. "Their team will play their best game against us," he continued. He had his squad feeling so sorry for the other team and coach that, subsequent to a defeat of them, one really felt remorse.

Coach Mears periodically read notes he claimed came from other schools criticizing our program and style of play. Some of the letters contained salty language. Doubting the authenticity of the correspondence, no one witnessed the post-marked envelopes. However, Coach apparently received a lot of mail from the Kentucky side.

Coach Mears accused other schools of sending people undercover to spy on his practices. Assuredly, anyone who entered the gym unauthorized was in for a total shakedown. During one of the Vol practice session, a hippie wandered in sporting long hair, torn jeans, sandals, and a T-shirt with a large peace sign on the front. Coach Aberdeen stopped this intruder yelling, "Chicken footer." (That is what Aberdeen labeled individuals wearing the peace sign because the symbol did look like a chicken foot.) Stopping the drills, Coach Aberdeen interrogated this guy like he was working for the CIA, but the poor fellow was only taking a short cut on his way to his next class.

Coach Mears believed firmly that Kentucky was spying on him. In preparation for a game with the Cats the Vols' All American Ron

Widby collided with Bill Young, resulting in an injury to Widby's shooting hand. The coaching staff used the utmost care to make sure the injury was kept concealed. They even admitted Ron to the hospital under an alias—David Bell. When the team traveled to Lexington, Ron walked into Pat Riley, one of Kentucky's stellar players. Pat asked Ron, "How's your hand; are you going to play tonight?" Even though great pains had been taken to secure the secret, in Widby's case the scheme had leaked to the Cats. Perhaps Mears thought someone at the hospital was working undercover for the boys of the Bluegrass State.

Before every practice, both home and away, Mears would send his team managers and other personnel on an all-out scouting mission of the facilities. From time to time the scouts returned with a prisoner. Such was the case in Lexington during the Bill Justus era when deputized manager Greg Coffman and sportswriter Marvin West found a Kentucky spy hiding underneath the bleachers while attempting to steal the Vols' game plan. The episode played during the Mear's Era was comparable to *007, I Spy, The Fugitive*, and *Mission Impossible* all rolled into one and it was quite a show.

Before the WCW

 A lot of halftime performers came down the pike at Tennessee during the Mears Era, but the most memorable involved Vol player, Roger Peltz. Roger was the headliner for Mears' program. Seeing little action in games, he was as invaluable to Mears as some of the key players.

Of course, if you have a good team or a superb player, fans will buy tickets, but at Tennessee Coach Mears had something extra special. He had winning teams, plus he had the clown that every circus would envy in Peltz. Mears wanted people not only to enjoy the game, but he wanted the people to enjoy themselves, laugh, and have a great time so they would return to the "big top" whenever it was in town. This is why during one Vol classic tournament he introduced a half-time show with Roger Peltz wrestling a black bear. That night the game was almost the sideshow, and Peltz the headliner. Prior to the event, Mears had posters tacked everywhere: "Peltz vs. the Bear; Who Will Survive?" Tennessee could have sold 30,000 tickets that night.

The bear had Peltz pinned a couple of times to the point where you could barely see the Vol underneath. However, Roger gave the bear all he wanted, but in the end the Vol performer was just glad to be alive. The crowd thought the performance was hilarious. Before the WCW there was Roger vs. the bear at Stokely, and what a great night for entertainment it was!

Don't Send Me to the Training Room

 While participating in the athletic program at UT, players dreaded being sent for a visit with the head trainer and his assistant. I really believe they could have possibly treated the wounded during the Civil War, and sometimes I think that some of their training philosophies originated in the great conflict. A common diagnosis could result in the following remark: "Son, the best thing to do is leave the injury alone; it will heal naturally." Basketball players hated to go to that room so much at times it took three men to drag them down the hall.

Customarily when you arrived at the treatment room, the head trainer would greet you with the personality of a rattlesnake. He liked to open with the query: "What's wrong with you, boy?" Subsequent to your response, he might ask the question: "What sport?" At this point if your life was on the line you were going to die, especially if you did not say that holy word—*football.*

Football players got priority but everybody else fell into line and I mean literally fell if it was a leg or ankle injury. In that room you could observe footballers in whirlpools, footballers being given massages to injured areas, or footballers being wrapped. However, basketball players had a treatment all their own. Coach Mears must have had us on the lowest of insurance plans in the training room because regardless of the injury the trainers would get out an ice pack and say, "Boy, put it on the ankle and keep it there until the swelling goes down." The miracle drug in the UT training room was ice.

The whole time I was at UT I can only recollect one major injury—Jimmy Woodall's shoulder dislocation. I would be willing to bet "Big Jim" got ice therapy before he was rushed to the hospital and put in traction. Coach Mears used to brag, "Our players are mentally tough; we play even when we're injured."

Heck, we played when suffering pain to avoid the UT training room therapy.

The Mouse Is Loose

Stu Aberdeen, probably one of the fieriest assistant coaches in UT basketball history and one of the most colorful, was given a nickname during the NIT in 1971. A New York sportswriter labeled him the "Field House Mouse." Coach Aberdeen did not appreciate the term "mouse" which implied smallness Even though he was petite in stature, Coach's thought pattern was "big."

About every sentence that emerged from his mouth had the word "big" in it. For instance, "Son, you are a big-time player; this team needs to think big" or "Jimmy, that was a big-time play you made." Coach just did not like anything small and he especially disliked his name being used in a diminutive context. It was rumored that even though he was a graduate of Tusculum College, he forbade that fact be printed in the basketball brochure because Tusculum was a "small" school. Not only did Stu think big, in the NIT in 1972 he became a big actor.

It was Tennessee vs. Duke in Madison Square Garden and the game was tight down the stretch with both teams exchanging baskets. Nineteen thousand, five hundred fans awaited the outcome. Just as the momentum seemed to be changing in the Vols' direction, a questionable call was made on the court and Coach Aberdeen went ballistic. Coach had a tendency to let all the game energy accumulate inside him, and sometimes in a controversial situation he would vent it all out. When he released his venom, it was non-stop lip action. Coach had the metabolism of a hummingbird, and when he was chewing out an official, his mouth moved as fast as his heart beat.

On that questionable call in the NIT, Coach ran onto the court, voicing his displeasure. He barely crossed the sideline when the eastern official signaled the most perfect "T" with his hands, thinking it would stop the charge of Coach Aberdeen. But Stu was just warming up. He got in the official's face and was blasting him like some people might scold a yard dog. The official, slowly stepping to the scorer's table with Coach in hot pursuit, informed the scorer that he called a "T" on "Red." Aberdeen overheard the official call our team "Red." He had been calling us "Red" all night instead of "Orange." When Coach heard "Red," he responded in a flash: "Red? It's orange! How in the blankety-blank can you call the blankety-blank game if you're colorblind? You're not only colorblind; you're just plain blind!" Finally, with all the abuse this official could endure, he looked at Stu authoritatively and signaled another technical foul on "Red." At that point everyone was restraining Coach Aberdeen from the official except the "Big Orange" mascot.

The Volunteer team lost all their momentum as one Duke player after another went to the free throw line. They shot so many free throws one could have assumed they were shooting for teddy bears at the county fair. The shooting display was like a free throw clinic. As Vol players drank several cups of Gatorade, the Blue Devil marksmen continued their shooting and the unrelentless Coach kept jawing. It was quite a sight; when they finished shooting, the Vols' chance of winning the game had faded. Coach Aberdeen's tirade left the official with a clean pair of ears and earned Stu the reputation of the "Field House Mouse."

Spittin' Hawkers

After our freshmen game with Florida, I sat near the Tennessee bench to watch the varsity game and got a very good dose of what Alligator Alley was all about. The Vols had lost a road game at Georgia the previous Saturday night and this game was crucial for Southeastern Conference survival.

Seated directly behind Coach Mears were several Florida football players who were distinguished by their necks, which were non-existent. Looking like a head had just been attached to their shoulders, they were huge, hostile, vocal, and exhibited some of the most corrupt manners I have ever witnessed. During the game they yelled obscene remarks at the Tennessee players like, "Little Jimmy England, are you on the training table? If you are, they're not feeding you enough." Their remarks became more pungent and their actions became increasingly deplorable as the game progressed.

Coach Mears was seated directly in front of the footballers that were located in stands similar to a high school gym, with little space between the bench and the fans. This group of football players took their harassment to an all-time low by spitting on the back of Coach Mears' orange blazer who was unaware of the situation as he was so involved in the game. One hawker after another made a direct hit.

The Vols lost the contest on a controversial tip in, and following the game in the locker room the front of Coach's coat was orange and the back was white from the hawkers' spit. The blazer was going to be a dry-cleaner's nightmare. Such was life at Alligator Alley for Ray Mears and the Tennessee Vols.

A Premature Judgment

During the Ray Mears Era there was never enough room in Stokely Athletic Center to seat everybody. All permanent seats (12,700) were sold out in either season tickets or allotted to the students. To put a few more fans in the house, the athletic department placed fold-up chairs around the court. These seats were filled with special requests given to Coach Aberdeen the week prior to the game.

On the night we played Alabama during my junior year my future mother-in-law occupied one of these seats located on the front row directly behind the basketball goal. During the game while conversing with some of the fans seated nearby, she mentioned that her daughter was dating me. As the game progressed, the inquisitive fans asked a few questions about me. Unhesitatingly, her assessment was that I seemed "like a nice young man who had always exhibited impeccable character" in her presence. Soon after this personal evaluation, the basketball came loose directly under the goal; I dove in an attempt to retrieve it when it ricocheted off my arm and out of bounds. In frustration, I blurted out, "Well, I'll be a son-of-a-bitch!" Disappointedly, my mother-in-law-to-be turned to the fans seated next to her and quickly added, "Until now."

A Lost Cause

It was during the 1970-71 season the expectations for the Vol program were starting to look up. The coaching staff had signed a six-foot, eleven-inch transfer from the University of Cincinnati, and part of the excitement came from the fact that the tallest player at UT at the time was six-foot, five-inch Jim Woodall. The player that was going to take the Vols to a new level had arrived. Quite intimidating, he was strong and possessed muscular legs, appearing to have the potential of an All American.

Coach Aberdeen took pride in preparing big men to attain their full capability, and he had done a marvelous job with Tom Boerwinkle, Jim Woodall, and later Len Kosmalski. He saw this highly touted player as just another challenge. Well, he was more than a challenge; he was a coach's nightmare.

This coach's challenge operated at one speed—slow; and even though he had the huge pair of hands, he could not catch the ball proficiently. Coach Aberdeen would yell and scream in an attempt to motivate him to speed up, to get aggressive, and to go all out, but the player's philosophy was, "I'll rest today and work tomorrow." The problem was tomorrow never came. Hard work was not in his vocabulary, so his days at UT under Coach Mears were numbered.

Assistant Coach Gerald Oliver tried to motivate him during pre-season practice; but one morning when Coach Oliver came to the dormitory to arouse the players for an early morning workout, the unmotivated Vol locked himself in his closet. Coach Ollie had a difficult time getting him out.

The player never saw action in any Tennessee varsity games, and his basketball career ended when he made some ill-fated decisions. Coach Mears believed that the integrity of the program was to be upheld above any individual. As a result the transfer from Cincinnati lost an opportunity to play for a great coach at an outstanding university.

Money Heals

During the 1971 NIT in New York City, ORU, founded by faith healer Oral Roberts, was invited to the tournament. At the conclusion of a Tennessee practice session during the NIT, Coach Mears was interviewed by some of the local sportswriters. One of the inquisitive writers asked, "How can a school like Oral Roberts University organize a new basketball program and make it to the NIT in such a short period of time?" While rubbing his fingers and thumb together, Coach Mears responded: "Money heals."

Twister

As a player I was very emotional and highly competitive. I don't know where this characteristic originated, but perhaps it was a result of my Indiana basketball heritage and the emphasis placed on winning. Nevertheless, I developed this orientation that losing was never acceptable and when it occurred it took me a long time to recover—about three or four days.

Subsequent to losing a game during my high school career I would walk the streets of my hometown while assessing the contest for all hours of the night. I continued this practice while at UT. Basketball and basketball alone consumed all my thoughts. Upon losing I was miserable and I made darn sure everyone around me was also. Fortunately, I had only a few losing experiences to endure during my career; nonetheless, the ones that did occur were nights to remember.

During my freshman year when Georgia was the Vol opponent, I recall one of those nights. Playing a tight game, the Vols lost on a questionable call in the closing seconds. For some reason we had dressed in our game uniforms at the motel and a university classroom served as our locker room. This proved to be a big mistake. Upon entering the room after the game, I began my other ritual after a loss—throwing things. I began hurling desks and chairs in every direction against the walls, doors and windows. With about thirty to thirty-five chairs in that room, not one was standing erect when I vented my frustration. Creed Daniels, a Morristown attorney who was traveling with the team, entered the room and had to duck one of the pitched chairs. I remember his astonished reaction vividly: "What the hell is going on? What has hit this place? It looks like a twister has come through here."

I did not see Creed after I ended my career at UT, but I talked to others to whom he had related this story through the years. Eruptions were fairly common in my playing days among coaches and players but today you would be labeled crazy and forced to enroll in anger management courses. At today's standards during the Mears Era at

UT perhaps the whole coaching staff and half the players would have been required to attend counseling sessions. If remediable measures had been mandatory at that time, I doubt if Mears would have ever won over seventy percent of his games, and poor Coach Aberdeen would probably have spent the majority of his life in the Tennessee State Prison swinging his broom at bats. But, hey, it was a different time!

Getting Trimmed

During off-season the University of Tennessee basketball staff conducted a program for young people in the summer labeled "The Camp of Champions." The youngsters were transported via bus from Knoxville to Arden, North Carolina, where the enrollees quickly discovered it was not a Boy Scout or YMCA Camp. It was a rigorous basketball camp under the direction of UT Assistant Coach Stu Aberdeen.

The campers lived, slept, and ate basketball. It was merely an extension of the "Big Orange Program." Instruction and games were conducted in scorching hot gyms or outside on asphalt courts. Aberdeen even desired a triple elimination tournament on the final day of camp. The tournament could last up to twenty-four hours, depending on who won and who lost. Even rain would not prevent the tournament games as several teams battled through thunderstorms and hail to qualify for the winners' bracket. Coaches would yell instructions from under umbrellas. Dribbling became a lost art under the rainy conditions because there were too many puddles to avoid. But all through the day one could hear the fiery Aberdeen hollering encouragement as if it were mid-season. "It's a great day, big guy, for you to get better; it's a good chance to experience playing in the rain"; or "first is first and second is last."

Aberdeen and the Tennessee staff stressed the importance of physical appearance of the athletes, which entailed the wholesome All-American look—no facial hair of any kind, a nice trim haircut, and neat clothes. They advocated that one's appearance portrayed the way he performed.

Well, when Coach Aberdeen took the Vol program on the road to Arden for the "Camp of Champions," the same philosophy prevailed. Now this camp was held in the sixties and early seventies when revolts were erupting to protest the Vietnam War. Rebellious students expressed their rights by wearing their hair long, and it was not uncommon to observe long hair on men anywhere you went except at Stu's camp.

When the campers got off the bus after their long trip from Knoxville, the first person they met was Coach Aberdeen. He checked every camper's hair for the proper length and if it did not pass his inspection, back on the bus they went. Sometimes there could be up to ten campers who did not meet coach's standards. Some had the Goldilocks appearance that evidently made their mom's proud. Upon completing the inspection, Aberdeen ordered the bus driven to the local barbershop so all the longhaired campers could attain a new look.

The barbers in Arden must have looked forward to Coach Aberdeen's arrival. He was a stickler when it came to proper hair length. If he felt it was getting too long, he made no comments but would pull hair from behind. It was then you better get a cut or your butt would be on the baseline for the demanding "suicide" drill the next day. Even today when my hair gets a little long I think of Coach Aberdeen.

Anybody Speak German?

Coach Aberdeen was speaking to a group of young basketball campers at Maryville College; and while he was talking, one of the campers proceeded to converse with his friend. The longer Coach spoke, the louder this camper got. Periodically Coach Aberdeen stopped speaking and gave the lad that meltdown stare for which he was so famous. Apparently fearless of the highly competitive coach, the youngster ignored the warning stare by continuing to "visit" with his friend.

Tolerating the camper's behavior no longer, Aberdeen took the basketball he was holding and threw it at the boy, striking him directly in the side of the head. The whole gym became silent with each camper afraid to move. However, the lad who took the hit looked up with amazement and continued to talk. Coach headed toward him, determined to make his point more clear. Before he reached the boy, I grabbed Coach and said, "This boy is a foreign exchange student from Germany and he speaks no English." The extremely embarrassed coach headed directly to the poor boy to check out the damage. The right side of the lad's face appeared to have tire tracks on it and it was as red as an apple. I can assure you that Coach attempted to apologize in German, but it sounded like a cross between Latin and Spanish to me.

However, Coach must have been successful in his attempt to apologize; subsequent to this incident, the young German lad impressed Coach Aberdeen with the toughness he displayed and the two became best friends.

String Music and a Butt Full of Foot

On Saturdays the televised Southeastern Conference game of the week was aired with Joe Dean. Joe had been an outstanding basketball player at LSU and later became the school's athletic director. Each week as an outside jumper went through the goal, basketball fans could hear Joe blurt out his trademark phrase: "He played a little string music in Knoxville, Tennessee." Joe did a lot to promote the conference, giving it some national prominence, which previously had been lacking.

Through the years Joe Dean witnessed the change in attitude of young players. This change was quite evident during summer basketball camps he conducted for youngsters. One summer a young lad attended that was extremely undisciplined, causing considerable turmoil for the other campers. A "bad egg," the camper's behavior became very stressful to Joe who even tried counseling the youngster, but to no avail. One day Joe asked the boy to apologize to another camper for trying to pick a fight; but the boy sassed the camp director, so Joe kicked him in the butt.

The parents of the boy sued Joe Dean and he was required to go to court to explain to a judge what had happened. After several days of testimony, the court ruled that Joe was guilty of the alleged act and was assessed a fine plus court costs. After reading the verdict, the judge asked, "Mr. Dean, have you got any regrets for kicking this child?" to which Joe replied, "I surely do; I wish that I had kicked him twice because he was a two-butt-kick kid."

The Scoop

 Two renowned sportswriters covered basketball in the local Knoxville newspapers during the Mears Era—Ben Byrd of *The Knoxville Journal* and Marvin West of *The Knoxville News-Sentinel*. There were other sportswriters like Ed Harris and Tom Siler, but football was their forte.

While the Vols were fighting for a southeastern conference championship, these two guys wrote columns about football. They were twelve-month-a-year football reporters. Tennessee would be playing Kentucky in basketball for the number one spot in the conference, but on the day of the game Siler and Harris would reminisce about what happened in the 1925 Tennessee-Vandy football game or the long run made by George Cafego. Rarely did either of them attend a basketball game.

Ben Byrd was known as the gentle writer. He reported the game as he saw the action and used the utmost patience in censuring a coach or player. When Ben reached a state of criticism you could rest assured the player or coach was on his way out. He was superb in his analysis and reporting

Marvin "Scoop" West was on the opposite end of the spectrum. He believed that controversy sold papers so he constantly searched for a scoop—hence his nickname. Coach Mears used to say that if the squad were winning and were in the penthouse, Marvin could write a column that would make them feel they were the greatest of all time; however, if the team lost and made the drop to the outhouse, "Scoop" would describe the Vols in a hopeless state.

An expert at observing an individual's emotions, Marvin would attend practice and if he saw a player exhibit frustration in any way, that Volunteer could expect a phone call in his dorm room that night. A young athlete had to exercise the utmost caution in expressing his feelings; otherwise, the next day the headline in the sports section might read: "Player Upset with Coaching Staff and UT Program." "Scoop" printed any remark that pertained to the situation. Coach Mears was quoted many times based on emotional states, and Marvin was a professional at utilizing remarks during stressful events. West could express great empathy with players or staff when confronting them as a scheme he used for a "roast" the next day in his sports column.

At times when players saw Marvin coming, they would retreat in the opposite direction. Most Vol basketballers realized that an insensitive statement made during a stressful experience printed by a sportswriter could result in severe consequences at practice the next day.

Ben Byrd's and Marvin West's scoops helped enhance the spectacle Tennessee basketball became during the Mears Era

How Not to Put on a Coat

During the 1969-70 season Ray Mears and his Volunteers went to Auburn to play the Tigers in a key Southeastern Conference game. As the result of an erratic season for Mears' troops, the coach was feeling a little more pressure than usual. Earlier in the year they had lost three consecutive games to Georgia, Florida, and Kentucky; that was very unusual for Mears' boys, and they could not afford another loss against Auburn. In fact, it was a do-or-die game, according to Coach.

The first half of the contest was very close and as it came to a conclusion, the fireworks started. Coach Mears was not pleased with the play of his team. There had been too many mistakes made on the floor both from a mental and physical standpoint. Just as the final seconds ran off the clock a "no call" by the official resulted in a mistake by a Volunteer player that resulted in an Auburn basket. This sent Coach Mears over the edge.

He took off his orange blazer, walked to the far end of the bench where Ken Rice, a basketball booster, was seated and sat down in disgust, minus the blazer. He was still steaming when the halftime buzzer rang and he obviously forgot that when he took the blazer off in his anger he had turned it inside out. Now Coach never wore anything with orange on the inside but on this occasion he did. All the coat's inside pockets and seams were showing. As coach put the coat on and walked off the court, he exited the arena with the fire of a pit bull. At least the orange portion of the coat was closest to his heart.

After the game, Dickie Johnston asked Jimmy England in the locker room, "Did you see that?"

Lights, Cameras, Action

 The Vols had just finished being humiliated by an Al McGuire-coached basketball team at Marquette and were approaching their locker room when a commotion occurred.

Seven-foot center Len Kosmalski had picked up with both hands the Warriors' manager, who stood about the size of a leprechaun; to make matters worse, Kos proceeded to give the diminutive fellow a tongue-lashing. A giant of a man, Kos held this runt of a kid three feet off the floor; the scene could have depicted an episode from a movie portraying David and Goliath or the Giant vs. Jack in the Beanstalk fable.

Nevertheless, Kos, assuming the Warrior was not getting the message he was attempting to convey, decided to take further action by sailing him through some nearby windows. It was a Hollywood moment—one of the best action scenes in Tennessee basketball history. As the manager crashed through the glass, Kos released some frustration. It was a mighty brief scene, however, as someone "cut" any further action by restraining Kos.

The incident was probably precipitated by the manager's comment, which provoked the big guy from Tennessee. Most athletes, after suffering a loss, undergo a low toleration level—and especially giants.

The Wall

 During pre-season practice Coach Aberdeen implemented a drill that separated the men from the boys. Lining up the players along the bleacher wall, he required them to jump with both feet and touch the wall with outstretched arms and hands. It sounds like a simple enough procedure, but it was tough.

Beginning with a two-minute workout, he eventually required the squad to endure up to ten minutes. If a player stopped at any time, he needed to be prepared to take coach's verbal wrath. Some team members headed for the puke buckets which coach had placed around the court just to get a reprieve from the wall. Most of the players would endure the first two minutes or so but after that there was a lot of hanging on that wall.

A firm believer that the wall was where champions were made, Coach would move from one player to the next, patting them on the butt and trying to encourage them to put forth the maximum effort. Some players would have puddles of perspiration under their feet at the conclusion of the drill. If a Vol made it the entire ten minutes without stopping and had conquered the wall, he had beaten the odds. Respect for each other was a direct result of the wall.

The Vols were in the hunt for SEC championships on a regular basis, so the wall might have been the drill that made the difference. It was certainly not a drill for the weak at heart.

Burt and the Colonel

After completing a grueling practice in the Los Angeles sports complex in preparation for a game in the Trojan Classic, the Volunteer squad were leaving the building. We saw several police cars and what appeared to be a television film crew in the tunnel below the arena. Assuming an accident had occurred, we approached the scene but learned that a segment was being filmed for the TV series entitled "Dan August," a detective story starring Burt Reynolds. When the famous actor noticed our orange blazers, he walked over to our team and asked what school we represented. Sharing some experiences with us, he related that he had played football at Florida State and really enjoyed college sports. He invited us to hang around and observe the scene being shot. He stated: "We've been shooting this same segment since 8 a.m.; you'd think after fifty thirty-second takes the director would find one that would be acceptable." That comment by Burt reminded me of the times we ran our offensive patterns over and over in practice that day. The big difference, however, was that Burt was to be recompensed liberally for his strenuous endeavors; we would be fed supper.

On this same trip we encountered a very distinguished elderly gentleman entering his hotel room. Further investigation confirmed the white-haired man was Colonel Harland Sanders of Kentucky Fried Chicken fame in Los Angeles to film a commercial for the company. A personable celebrity, the Colonel during our brief chat readily displayed his unique wristwatch that contained diamonds at the second digits and numbers positions. Not to be outdone, I proudly showed him the Wyler watch each of our team members had been awarded for playing in the Volunteer Classic. Not impressed, however, the Colonel never mentioned a possible trade.

Swim, Anyone?

 Volumes could be filled with Stu Aberdeen stories. Everyday was an incredible journey with the Volunteer assistant dynamo. It was late October and the afternoon air was downright cold, but to Coach Aberdeen it was another great day to improve our physical and mental prowess..

On this pre-season day he decided to work on the mental aspect of the game. Taking the team to the outdoor aquatic center pool, Coach ordered the squad to run sprints across the shallow end of the pool. Now the water was just a shade warmer than the Atlantic Ocean the night the Titanic sunk, but Coach Aberdeen reasoned it would only feel cold upon first entering and the body would get acclimated to it. After two minutes in that water, most players experienced numbness from the waist down. Doctors could have amputated both legs minus an anesthetic. The Vols raced back and forth across that pool in relay style and no team was permitted to exit the water until the last player finished. Enduring this ordeal while wearing the orange practice gear, the squad had attracted quite a crowd by the time they had finished. No doubt most onlookers concluded total insanity had set in on campus.

Coach enjoyed every second of the challenge. Doubting if it really accomplished making us more mentally tough, I can assure you I never entered a cold pool again.

Anyone Thirsty?

During practice sessions only one Gatorade break was permitted. The practices lasted three and one-half hours with a recess coming at the two-hour mark; this custom resulted in two hours of rugged play without any fluid replacement to the body.

Now Coach was really proud of that Gatorade. He even told recruits that they would be offered Gatorade instead of water during practices. The problem was he reckoned it so valuable that only a small portion was allotted. In fact, he even had it guarded, appointing David "General" Mills, the manager, and his staff with that responsibility. Counting it a unique drink promoting the Vol big orange trademark, Coach Aberdeen even changed the name of the liquid to Vol-ade.

Half way through practice and after we shot our twenty-five free throws, we all raced to the Vol-ade container. A free-for-all erupted with players pushing one another to obtain a cup. Picking up the small cups, we could not decide whether to drink from it or to deposit a urine specimen in it. We had barely filled our little cup when Coach Aberdeen blew the whistle to commence the last half of practice and the dreaded defensive drills.

Many coaches in the sixties theorized that drinking a lot of fluids resulted in players getting sick and losing their edge. A player who craved water on a consistent basis was not considered mentally tough. Times have changed since then and fluids are freely dispensed when a player desires them. Reminiscing how hard it was to get a cold drink during those tough practices, I really appreciate a cold beverage today, and, of course, I always choose an extra large cup.

I Can See My Breath

On a cold wintry morning in Indiana a group of sixty basketball fans from my hometown of Greenfield, Indiana, boarded a chartered bus heading to Knoxville, Tennessee, to see the Vols play. With high spirits they were looking forward to an exciting weekend. However, thirty miles into the trip disaster struck. The heating system on the bus malfunctioned, and the fans had to ride the next three hundred miles in freezing temperatures. Heavy coats, blankets, hot chocolate, and coffee became a necessity for survival.

I always knew my hometown was a close-knit community but nothing compared to the closeness exhibited on this cold bus as everyone huddled to keep warm. In spite of the near calamity, the bus did arrive in time for our encounter with Alabama and all on board survived. They witnessed a spine-tingling basketball game that went down to the last shot with the Vols winning. Apparently my hometown fans never got warm during the lively rivalry, however, as some viewed the contest while still wrapped in their coats.

No Tickets, No Problem

 It was Tennessee vs. Kentucky in a key UT showdown in Stokely and the arena as usual was a sell-out. There were no tickets to be found anywhere; apparently the entire state of Kentucky and Tennessee coveted tickets.

John Heatherly, who was an outstanding baseball coach at Farragut High School in Knoxville, Tennessee, and a great individual, had a friend who called him regarding them attending the game together. John emphasized to his friend that tickets to the game were non-existent and that he did not possess even one. His persistent friend said, "Don't worry about it; we'll get in. I'll pick you up at 6:30 p.m."

John, assuming his buddy had two tickets, discovered that was not the case. Upon their arrival at the arena, the Farragut baseball coach followed his friend who headed directly to an usher before whom he flashed a FBI badge. Stating that he and Heatherly were working undercover to locate an individual that had made threats and was expected to be in attendance at the game, they were waved on into the arena with no questions asked. John and his buddy worked under cover all right—from the third row aisle at mid court.

George Wallace—the Pilot

 During the early part of the Ray Mears Era the Vol Basketball Team flew on the University airplane nicknamed "The General" that was piloted by George Wallace. No, he did not become governor of Alabama; this George Wallace was a pilot only.

Some Vols expressed an uneasy feeling while flying on the General, thinking every trip on the aged aircraft might be their last. On one foggy night as the General approached the Knoxville Airport subsequent to a Vol victorious road trip, this feeling could have become a reality. Pilot George was faced with a low fog that made locating the runway very tricky. In fact, Wallace was so concerned that he made a couple of approaches to verify his calculations When planes start circling, passengers get nervous, and the Vol players were no exception, especially when no ground could be seen.

Finally, George decided it was time to bring the General down, so he started the descent. The plane went down and down but there was still no sign of the ground. Just as the players thought the plane was not going to land, an object was seen ahead and a sigh of relief was heard. But the relief was short lived as the object came into view: It was the control tower at the Knoxville Airport. Heading straight for it, at the last second Wallace took a hard right, avoiding putting the General out of commission, not to mention the Vol Basketball Team.

Some team members when asked an assessment of the potential disaster remarked, "You could see the whites of the controllers' eyes in the tower." Others vowed, "You could see the controllers backs as they were running." George Wallace finally landed the plane on that dismal night and a Vol memory was etched forever.

The Orange Slice

Coach Mears had been informed of the rule change from the NCAA office that no dunking would be permitted on the court during warm-ups or during the game. Any infraction of this rule would result in a technical foul. This rule came into effect in the latter 1960's, primarily as a result of the increasing number of taller and bigger players. Also, our present-day breakaway rims did not yet exist. When players dunked the ball, rims were bent and torn off; in some cases entire backboards were shattered. The non-dunking rule change was not popular with fans; and Coach Ray Mears certainly did not enthusiastically accept it either. At the time he boasted one of the few big centers in the country, Bobby Croft, who had featured dunking the ball in Coach's Globetrotter warm-up drills.

Always a step ahead of his opponents, Coach Mears figured out a solution to the problem. He took a portable fan-shaped backboard and goal, had it mounted on a frame and rolled it out in front of the main goal. He also ordered it painted to mimic a huge orange slice. The rule stated no dunking on the main goals but did not mention portable goals. What a basketball genius Coach was—always ahead of his time whether it be offensive or defensive strategies or planning his famous warm-ups! He even set the height of the rim at eight feet so that the smallest man on his squad, Dickie Johnston, could bring the crowd to their feet with a tomahawk dunk.

With Roger Peltz riding a unicycle and juggling three balls at one time and the Vols dunking on an orange-slice backboard, the "circus" was at the height of its glory and performed before packed houses.

He Only Took Orders from a Higher Power

Tommy Hendrix, better known as "Spook" by his teammates, was a great player at the University of Tennessee and was also an outstanding performer in the basketball-rich state of Kentucky. In fact, during his senior year in high school he was labeled the number two player in the entire state, catching the eye of the "Baron of the Bluegrass," Adolph Rupp.

It was at the state tournament at Freedom Hall in Louisville, Kentucky, that Adolph decided to offer Hendrix a scholarship to play for the Cats. Hendrix had led his team to the state tournament, and it was a proud moment for his hometown and especially his family.

At the conclusion of Tom's game at the tournament, Adolph located Tom's dad in the stands. He dispatched a representative from his staff to inform Mr. Hendrix that he wanted to discuss with him an offer for his son to play for the University of Kentucky. When the representative invited Mr. Hendrix to come up and sit with Coach Rupp to talk about the offer, Mr. Hendrix informed him, "If Adolph wants to talk to me about my son coming to his school, he can come down here to me."

Coach Rupp did not make the trip down to talk to Mr. Hendrix. In fact, Adolph never initiated any further overtures to Tommy. Coach Rupp only took his orders from a higher power.

I'm Stranded

Billy Justus, scheduled to play in the East/West All-Star Game in Indianapolis at the conclusion of his senior year in college, and Adolph Rupp, who would be coaching him in the game, happened to be on the same flight to Indy.

In fact, the Baron, seated next to Billy, began his spiel on the Kentucky basketball program to him all over again. Telling him what a great player he would have made for the Cats, Rupp chidingly related to Billy that if he had played the Kentucky style of basketball he could have been drafted higher in the pro's and made more money. Admonishingly Adolph stated: "That slow-down ball doesn't get anybody ready for the pro's."

He kept selling Billy the entire trip and what was so ironic was that Rupp never spent a lot of time recruiting any player, let alone someone whose eligibility had elapsed. Usually Rupp would check to see if the player was an All-State or an All-American athlete before he made a contact regarding his interest in coming to Kentucky. I recall that the Baron made one call when he recruited me and the same rule applied with Bill Justus and several other players.

Perhaps, for a Kentucky high school player one call from the Baron proved to be convincing; but for a kid from Indiana or Tennessee who considered Kentucky a big rival, one contact was probably insufficient. Customarily, Adolph only gave you one chance to play for the Cats.

Coach Rupp made the flight to Indianapolis and coached the game but had a slight problem afterwards. Since the contest lasted longer than he expected, Rupp missed his flight back to Kentucky. The Baron asked the P.A. announcer to make the following request: "Coach Rupp needs a ride back to Lexington; if anyone can help please meet him at the scorer's table." Coach Rupp waited a long time at the scorer's table but no one ever showed up. Probably the Baron forgot he was in Indiana, and Hoosiers are not too fond of "Bluegrassers."

Pre-Game Celebration

In 1969 the Tennessee Vols were invited to the National Invitational Tournament. A very close-knit team, the players were very excited about going to New York to play. The NIT accepted twenty-four teams at the time with the games being played in Madison Square Garden from morning to midnight. A squad had to be conference champions to qualify for the NCAA Tournament so the NIT had many teams that were capable of winning the national championship. The Vols were thrilled to be invited as the tournament was considered a milestone in any basketball player's career.

In fact, the squad was so elated that the night before leaving for New York, the staff called a midnight team meeting at Gibbs Hall. Several team members were married students and midnight was a little late for them, but when all arrived they picked each other up and threw one another into the shower in celebration. I thought the custom was to throw one another in the shower subsequent to a big win; however, this team had a different custom: throw everybody in the shower and then win.

The pre-tournament celebration must have worked because they came close to becoming the first Volunteer basketball squad to ever win a national tournament. They beat Bob Knight's Army team to finish third in one of the most prestigious tournaments in America.

Not Big but Quick

During his senior year at Fulton High School in Knoxville, Tennessee, Bill Justus was highly recruited by several schools. Kentucky was one of the schools interested, but their hands-off approach probably cost them Bill's services. Bill got one call from the Cats with a scholarship offer, and that was the extent of the recruiting procedure.

Coach Ray Mears, however, wanted the six-foot, three-inch wingman in the worst way. Bill, an outstanding student, exhibited exceptional basketball ability. Mears felt Justus would be perfect for his 1-3-1-offense system while playing the right wing. Justus was a superb shooter, and Coach Mears expected him to become the offensive scorer he needed. Furthermore, Bill was from Knoxville and losing him to another school, especially an SEC university, could be embarrassing for the UT basketball coaching staff. Coach Mears recruited Bill intensely, probably losing sleep until he convinced the Fulton Falcon to don the orange blazer.

In early January Coach Mears, his patience dwindling, decided to cut a deal with the football program, trading a basketball scholarship for a football scholarship. This would enable him to sign Justus in January instead of waiting until May. The plan worked; Billy signed with the Vols in January and was enrolled on a football scholarship his entire four years with Tennessee. Bill, lacking the physique of a football player, no doubt was glad the football staff never requested his services. But if they had, Justus would have endeavored to be useful because he is "big orange" all the way through. He probably would have told everybody, "I'm not very big, but I'm really quick."

Running through the "T"

During the introduction of the Vol's starting five, traditionally the team ran through a gigantic "T" with the benefit of a spotlight in a darkened arena. With orange paper placed on the opening of the "T," the seal was broken as the first in line burst through while entering the playing surface. It was quite a thrill to be first although I think most players preferred to be second. Not assured of what was on the other side of the paper, the first in line faced the risk of falling, and becoming entangled in the paper could cause your loss of balance.

Coach Mears was the first to utilize the power "T" for players to run through at UT; however, the custom actually originated with the Pep Club for students. (The club's official name was the Adawayhi Campus Pep Club with "Adawayhi" probably having some Cherokee reference.) Bill Justus claimed to have met the club member many years later that conceived the tradition. One of the novel customs of Volunteer sports history, the ritual has continued as various sports introduce their team and coaching staff in this manner today. The student body is and always will be a major part of the success of all the Volunteer sports programs.

The Garment Bag

When traveling on the road, the basketball Volunteers always flew first class. They chartered flights, stayed in the finest hotels, ate at the best restaurants and toured the famous sites in the large cities. The team, always wearing their orange blazers, toted an orange and white travel bag. The identification on the bag was unique, displaying the individual's picture.

The Vols' unique garment bag contained coats, pants, shirts and anything else that was susceptible to wrinkling. Proudly carrying the garment bag over their shoulders, the squad crossed many airport corridors and hotel lobbies. The Tennessee orange garment bag disclosed the player's name stitched at the top. On the back was this beautifully embroidered Tennessee shield in royal blue and gray with the word "Tennessee" placed at the top of it and "Volunteer" underneath. (Rumor was that a lady who lived in the Smokey Mountains embroidered the bags.) Coach Mears had the bag designed for promotional purposes. When the player placed it over his shoulder, all that was exposed was the orange side and "Tennessee Volunteers."

At the conclusion of my career I donated my garment bag to the Indiana Basketball Hall of Fame in New Castle, Indiana, where it will remain forever. When my Mom and Dad presented it to the Hall, they were told it was one of the most unusual pieces of memorabilia the organization had received. A part of the Hall's display on various occasions, the garment bag was another part of the Ray Mears Era that now provides a fond memory.

Wetting a Line

Many UT basketball players came from small towns in rural areas of the country where outdoor activities were a way of life. They liked to hunt, fish, swim, and hike. Whatever their hometown environment had to offer they made good use of it.

The recreational aspects of this area provided an enticement for many recruits. The Great Smokey Mountains and the many lakes and streams made the area a haven for the outdoorsman.

Tom "Spook" Hendrix and Bill Justus were two players that took full advantage of the Knoxville area's natural resources and have continued to be avid fishermen throughout their lives. I would like to accompany them some time; but they probably use a variety of lures—spinner baits, repalas, Texas rigs, Carolina rigs, and jitterbugs. I prefer live bait—you know, the kind that moves. (Most big-time fishermen will not allow me in their boats because the worms tend to soil the upholstery.) I like live bait because I can catch a lot of fish without dislocating my shoulder when throwing a lure. I really do not care how big the fish are, as long as I am catching some.

Tommy Hendrix liked the location of Gibbs Hall Dormitory because it was near the Tennessee River; and where there is water there are fish. Ole Tommy was known to go on a few fishing trips down to the river, and on occasion he would leave his lures in his tackle box and substitute them with some good old fashioned dough balls. Dough balls are great bait. You can catch some of the biggest and ugliest fresh water fish with them on the planet—carp and catfish. All you have to do is put the dough ball on the hook, throw it out into the water, let it sink to the bottom, wait for the monster fish to run with it, and reel them in—absolutely no skill required whatsoever. That's my kind of fishing, requiring no past experience.

Frequently, "Spook" would head to the Tennessee River and catch himself a real mess of catfish but usually just threw them back in. On one occasion when he caught several, he decided to keep them. Figuring other players were tired of hearing his stories regarding how many fish he had caught, "Spook" loaded up his seven or eight channel cat and headed back to the dorm. When he got there no one was around for him to show off his success. He did not want to walk back to the river to dump the fish so he decided to fill up the shower stall in the dorm restroom with water and let the fish swim around until someone arrived to see what he had caught. No doubt those fish felt real uncomfortable swimming in such clean water!

I Don't Want Him; You Take Him

One of the outstanding freshmen teams in UT basketball history was composed of Ron Widby, Tommy Hendrix, Wes Coffman, Mac Petty and Tom Boerwinkle. After graduating from Tennessee, Widby went on to play several seasons with the Dallas Cowboys as a punter, and Mac Petty as coach of Wabash College in Indiana won a national championship in basketball. Tommy Boerwinkle had several stellar seasons as a center for the Chicago Bulls.

But the real story is how Boerwinkle ended up at Tennessee. He originated from Independence, Ohio, and attended Millersburg Military Institute (MMI) in Kentucky. His senior year at MMI he was quite sick and played most of the year with Mono. Tom was an astounding seven-foot tall center with his height probably being his major asset. He was a slow runner; his stamina was quite poor; he could not jump very well; and he was not very coordinated. But Tom's mind was sound and zeroed in on basketball, and in America at the time there just were not many guys his size around.

Boerwinkle caught the eye of Adolph Rupp. The Baron, knowing very few had the talent to play at Kentucky, decided to do his good friend Ray Mears (who at the time played an ultra slow-down disciplined game), a favor by acquainting him with the unpolished post player. He called Coach Mears and said, "Ray, I've seen this boy, Tom Boerwinkle, play; he's a big boy. They say he's seven feet tall. Now, Ray, he can't play for me but I think he will fit right into your program."

Boy, Adolph, always the master, was going to send Ray Mears a seven-foot post player with no stamina who cannot run the court. The Baron, with delight, was probably thinking: "I can't wait to play Tennessee with my thoroughbreds against their mules."

One cannot be certain how Coach interpreted that call from Rupp, whether he thought Adolph was ridiculing his disciplined, slowdown game or whether the Baron was boasting that he could pick and choose his players. Regardless, the last laugh was on Adolph because Tom Boerwinkle became one of the "giants" of Tennessee basketball history. He reached All-American status and had several outstanding years in the pro's. From all of us in Big Orange Country, "Thanks, Adolph, for letting us have him."

Making Change Out of a Quarter

During the latter 1960's Coach Stu Aberdeen recruited and then signed one of the greatest basketball players that never played for the Vols, Spencer Hayward. Graduating from Pershing High School in Detroit, Michigan, he was an awesome talent. He could jump out of the gym and had moves that were smooth as silk. His jump shot was picturesque. Spencer just did not dunk the ball; he threw it down the goal like a softball without effort. His high school grades were satisfactory enough to come to UT but he had trouble with the ACT entrance exam that prohibited him from full acceptance.

To tell you how valuable Coach Mears thought Spencer was he had informed Bill Hann and Bill Justus that he was going to red shirt them both if he could get Spencer eligible. That's like sacrificing two players for one. Hayward was as good as Bernard King in that era. He may have been the best to have ever played for the Vols if things had worked out.

When Spencer played pick-up games, he insisted the scrimmage be played full court, not half court to which a lot of Vol players were accustomed. He could move up and down the floor tirelessly, leading fast breaks on many occasions. Coach Aberdeen used to tell the story that Spencer could stand flat-footed under the goal and take a quarter off the top of the backboard. Now, this would have been quite a feat and no one ever questioned Coach Aberdeen on it because he was the one slinging the broom in practice. I like to believe all stories so let's put the record straight. Spencer was the first basketball Vol to take the quarter off the top of the backboard standing flat-footed on a vertical jump. And as Coach Aberdeen used to say, "He could take the quarter and then make change."

When things did not work out, Spencer left UT and ended up at Detroit University via a junior college in Colorado. The coach at Detroit was Dick "ESPN" Vitale. In 1968 Spencer became the first junior college player to ever win an Olympic Gold Medal in basketball. At the conclusion of his pro career he was voted one of the top one hundred pro players of all time.

For Tennessee Spencer Hayward was one of the "greatest, if not the greatest, that never was" for the Volunteers.

Give Us Our Ball Back or Else

It is hard to believe that there is only one arena left in the SEC that the players of the Mears Era (1960's-early 1970's) played in and that is Memorial Gymnasium at Vanderbilt University. All the old places had their individual charm. There was the ringing of cowbells in the old gym at Mississippi State and the flipping of pennies at players at the old gym at the "Village on the Plain" at Auburn. There was the old army-barrack-looking building at Georgia and there was Alligator Alley in Florida that was really worse than being stranded in a real swamp. There was Adolph's house, Memorial Coliseum, at Kentucky where one year when they were playing the Vols the student body gave Rupp's runts a standing ovation all the way through their warm-ups. There was the armory at UT and later Stokely Athletic Center where fans came by the thousands to see Ray Mears and his globetrotting Vols.

All the edifices (except the one at Vanderbilt) have vanished, but the memoirs are still vivid, memories that have led to traditions and traditions that have led to championships, thanks to the old fieldhouses.

One year while Tennessee was warming up preparing to play Vanderbilt in Memorial Coliseum, the orange and white basketball got loose during the globetrotter drills and landed in the Vanderbilt student section. The perplexed Volunteer players just stood on the floor, contemplating whether to attempt to retrieve the ball; they were quite aware that their entering the student section at Vanderbilt would be much akin to entering a den of rattlesnakes. To say the least, it just was not a place for a UT basketball player.

When Coach Mears traveled to Vanderbilt he took as his escort Bill Skinner, an Olympic javelin thrower who always wore an orange blazer and served as Coach's bodyguard. Possessing a formidable personage, Bill gave the impression he would not endure much folly. When he saw the warm-up ball being playfully tossed about in the Vanderbilt student section, this feat fell under Bill's category of "folly." He walked briskly to the student section, crawled over several students, violently grabbed the student who possessed the ball, and then it was like time had stopped. Most of the Vol players thought this poor student's life was surely history. The crowd became silent, hoping the kid would not do the Vanderbilt thing— throw the ball at Skinner. However this student proved by his action that Vanderbilt University contained at least some bright students; he smiled and submissively ceded the ball to Bill Skinner with no questions asked.

Nod for a Championship

It was 1967 and Bill Justus had missed the front end of a one-on-one free throw to send the game at Mississippi State into a third overtime. It was a must-win game for the Vols as the SEC championship was on the line. Bill was a sophomore and Mississippi State was taking full advantage of the young Vol by placing a lot of pressure on him down the stretch. With seven seconds left in the third overtime, Justus was fouled again. He was either going to place championship rings on all his teammates or go into a fourth overtime.

Mississippi State called time out to let him ponder the situation. As Bill stood in the huddle, his eyes roaming behind the bench, he saw D. D. Lewis, an outstanding Mississippi State football player who later played with the Dallas Cowboys, making his way toward the bench. D. D. practically grew up at the Knoxville Boys' Club and he knew Bill well as they had played sports together at Fulton High School. At this moment total friendship prevailed over school loyalty. As Bill's eyes met D. D.'s the bulky Bulldog linebacker gave him a reassuring nod. The nod provided the impetus Bill needed to sink both free throws and the Vols took home a championship.

The Snake Gets Rattled

 Tennessee had lost a heartbreaking game to Vanderbilt in Nashville and the squads were moving across the court to congratulate one another. The Commodores had a former player, Bob Grace, nicknamed "Snake," who was a graduate assistant coach. Grace was from Hopkinsville, Kentucky, and was a good player in his day for the Commodores.

According to "Snake," Vol player Ron Widby approached him after the game and Bob reached out to shake the Tennessee All-American's hand and tell him he played a good game. Ron refused to shake it but, according to Widby, the "Snake" said something that offended him. Regardless, of what was said, a huge fight developed with fans becoming involved. Fists and bodies were being thrown from every direction. There was always the potential for an explosive situation to develop when Tennessee and Vanderbilt played during the Mears Era.

Off to the Salt Mines

Very few players during the early seventies got to participate in an international game unless they were invited to Olympic competition. In 1972 the Polish National Team came to Stokely Athletic Center for a contest against the Volunteers.

The game was labeled an exhibition and was played mostly for public relations; however, from Coach Mears' standpoint, the game was comparable to an SEC rivalry with the United States opposing another country (Poland).

In his pre-game speech Ray Mears was never fierier. Instead of telling his team that their coach was fighting for his career, as was usually the case, the talk was geared toward the Polish players. With intense rhetoric, Mears remarked. "We'll have to play our best game tonight because these Polish boys are fighting for their life. If they don't win, they know their destination is the Salt Mines. You boys have never been in a salt mine; there's nothing worse than a salt mine. A coal mine doesn't even compare."

I have never been in any mine and since I am claustrophobic, and have never had any intention of going to the center of the earth in a small tunnel, I was sympathetic for the Polish team if the end result of the game was not in their favor.

I had mixed emotions for this exposition, since the results meant little on our win/loss record.. Those poor boys from Poland would be going to a despicable place forever. Even today when I make homemade ice cream, I wonder if any of those players had anything to do with mining the salt I was using to make the ice cream harden.

Coach Mears made a big deal about exchanging gifts at half court before the game. We presented the Polish team a UT decal and an American flag and they reciprocated with a handshake. I was hoping for some type of memorabilia to remember the night, maybe a Polish sausage or something else but we got a handshake. I guess times were hard behind the Iron Curtain.

The Poles had a unique way of rejecting the official's call; they reacted by dropping to their knees, covering their ears, moving their head from side to side, and screaming. They definitely got the official's attention along with 12,700 Vol fans. Today, this type of conduct would earn your team two technical fouls, a league fine, and a reservation at a mental institution. Ray Mears' Vols and the Polish National Team provided an international flavor in Big Orange Country and a night to remember for all Tennessee basketball fans.

Those Smokey Mountain Dogs

A nightly ritual for Tennessee basketballers was a late night trip to the Smokey Mountain Market near the UT campus to get cheese dogs, chips, and a coke. It was rumored that Tom Boerwinkle could not sleep until he had his ample allotment of the nightly snack. Players would line up at the market Monday through Sunday all year long to purchase those famous hotdogs.

Tom Hendrix, the Vols' outstanding wingman, even liked to patronize the market prior to the game. The night the Vols played Michigan, Tom, deciding the green Jell-O he ingested at the 5 p.m. pre-game meal was not going to provide the energy needed for the game, furtively traveled to the market and loaded up on cheese dogs. "Spook" was slow-of-foot that night. When the coaches discovered he had sneaked to the market before the game, they utilized the next several practice sessions to improve his speed by working the cheese dogs out of his system. Smokey Mountain Market hotdogs and Tennessee basketball were a winning combination.

Preservation

Coach Mears was always looking for a way to be a challenger for the Southeastern Conference Championship. He had an exceptional group of young sophomores in Tom Hendrix, Tom Boerwinkle, Ron Widby, Wes Coffman, and Mac Petty.

To keep the group primed for a conference title run, he red shirted all the aforementioned players except Widby.

Coach Mears exercised great foresight and wisdom by red shirting this group that later won a Southeastern Conference Championship in 1967. Many coaches would not have been bold enough to red shirt an entire squad. Red shirting a player exhibits a total commitment by the player and the coach. A player performs five years in the program instead of four and agrees to relinquish his opportunity to participate in games for an entire year. Five years of Coach Mears with four-and-a-half-hour practice sessions and Coach Aberdeen thrown in for good measure, these players should have had an extension on their 1967 Championship Banner which read: "In recognition of valor beyond the call of duty."

"Blue Moon"

Mac Petty's pick-up team was playing Tom Boerwinkle's team in a scrimmage and Mac could not miss a shot. Every attempted shot went through the hoop, and big Tom who did not like to lose was getting more and more frustrated as his team got farther and farther behind. Suddenly Tom ended the scrimmage; he had seen enough of Mac's shooting clinic.

The next day Mac asked Boerwinkle if he was ready to scrimmage again, and seven-foot-center Tom replied, "Yeah, I'm ready to scrimmage All-American 'Blue Moon' Petty." The nickname stuck. Mac Petty, a great Tennessee player, became "Blue Moon" in an orange world.

Teeny-Bopper Top Cat

It is almost unbelievable that two Tennessee basketball players actually outscored the great Pistol Pete Maravich in a game, but Bill Justus in 1968 and Jimmy England in 1970 accomplished the feat. Each player scored twenty-nine points respectively to Pistol's twenty-one. What made the scoring accomplishment of these two players so phenomenal was that Maravich scored in the forties on a consistent basis, and Vol players were not known for high-scoring averages due to the team's deliberate style of play.

When Pete was a sophomore, *Sports Illustrated Magazine* ran a story on the Bengal Tiger entitled "Teeny-Bopper Top Cat." The story ran a week prior to the Tennessee game so Vol players were fired up to play Maravich. During the game Bill Justus, Billy Hann, and other Tennessee players took turns taunting the great Maravich by calling him "Teeny-Bopper" and "Cutie." At times Maravich would not run to the defensive end of the court. He would sandbag to mid court and when the Tiger defense rebounded the ball they would throw him a long pass so he could score an easy basket. Toward the end of the game Maravich, playing with four fouls and receiving a pass at half court, started driving for the basket for an easy two; then he stopped just before laying the ball in. The Vol nearest to him was Bill Justus. Bill expected Maravich to lay the ball into the basket, but instead the Pistol turned to Justus and remarked, "Here's two for you, Cutie." On the next trip down the floor, Maravich committed his fifth foul, and Justus gave him a parting remark, "And it will be the last two for you, Cutie."

Got to Save Myself

During a high school tournament game in Stokely Athletic Center in 1971, a riot occurred. Pictures were ripped off the wall and trophy cases were broken. The scene was quite perilous. A great example of Ray Mears' ability to promote his program was located in the lobby area of the arena. Life-sized plywood cutouts of Vol players were on display. Each player was in an action pose so that every fan entering the arena could experience the player up close.

When the riot broke out, Greg Hawkins, one of the Vol players, was in Gibbs Hall that was adjacent to Stokely Arena. Discovering what was happening, he remarked to other players, "I've got to get over there and save myself." Greg ran through the riot zone, located his giant cutout with the help of no one, and exerting all his strength he retrieved it. That night on the eleven o'clock news the "Hawk" was the headliner as he was seen by television viewers saving "himself."

Listening More and Talking Less

During my tenure at UT, I had a post-graduate course with Pat Head Summit, the great Lady Vol Basketball Coach. Starting her program at UT, she was facing financial difficulties. In fact, the Women's Basketball Team had to raise most of their money just to survive. Dr. Nancy Lay was the instructor of this class and there were three former football players from Troy State University in Alabama who were enrolled.

One day during a discussion in class in regard to Title IX, which placed women's sports on an equal basis with men, the three Troy State football players made the following comments: "It took men seventy years to get where they are, and women's sports should endure the same growing pains. Programs are not financed overnight. Women have no right to expect men to share their revenues."

I could see that Pat was not pleased with the footballer's philosophy, especially since she had to peddle Krispy Kreme Doughnuts just to buy gas to get to the next game. I remained silent, assuming that these Alabama boys lacked foresight to anticipate that sexual equality was becoming a reality in the sports world. History verifies it did not take women's sports seventy years to make the rise, and it surely did not take Pat Head Summit long to turn the Lady Vols into national champions.

I do not know where those Alabama boys are today, but they can relate the following to their grandchildren: "We once told Pat Head Summit at Tennessee that the women's program was not equal to the men's and didn't deserve equal attention or equal money. We really put her in her place." Perhaps those Alabama boys should have listened more and talked less.

(L-R) A.W. Davis, Marty Morris, Ray Mears, and Stu Aberdeen

Jim Woodall preparing for the pre-game warm-up

Don Johnson

Dickie Johnston

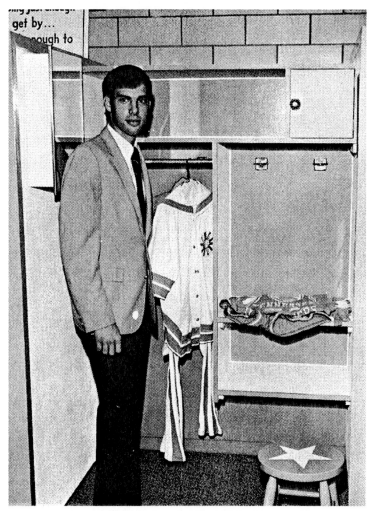

Jerry McClanahan in the Vol locker room

(L-R) Adolph Rupp, Stu Aberdeen, and Ray Mears

(L-R) Lloyd Richardson and Mike Edwards

Stokely Athletics Center on game night

Vols in the meeting room

Ken Rice—Mr. Loyalty

The Vol bench comes to life

A.W. Davis rebounding

John Snow drives against Kentucky

Tom Boerwinkle

(L-R) Howard Bayne, Red Robbins, A.W. Davis, and William Stokely (center)

(L-R) Clair Bee and Stu Aberdeen

Danny Schultz

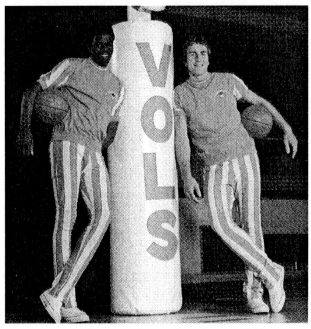

(L-R) Bernard King and Ernie Grunfeld

Mike Jackson

Bernard King hits the impossible shot against Kentucky

1967 Vol family celebrate a SEC Championship

Larry Robinson

John Ward—The Voice of the Vols

(L-R) Jimmy England and Don Johnson collect Vol Classic hardware

Bill Justus celebrates after hitting game-winning shot to defeat Florida

Larry Robinson runs through the "T"

Rodney Woods

Eddie Voelker

Len Kosmalski

Steve Hirschorn

The Ray Mears Show (L to R): John Ward, Coach Mears, and Ben Byrd

Ernie Grunfeld and Bernard King with the SEC Championship Trophy

Vols celebrate a great win over Kentucky

Orb Bowling

Dr. Andy Holt, former UT President

Howard Bayne

Coach Aberdeen questions an official

Bill Hann

Tom Hendrix

Wes Coffman

Tennessee Cheerleaders perform

Skip Plotnicki

Pat Robinette

Ron Widby

(L to R) Steve Hirschorn, Mike Edwards, Lloyd Richardson, Wayne Tomlinson and Len Kosmalski

Mike Edwards

Who's Slowing the Game Down?

 Every player that an opposing coach would recruit would tell the boy, "Don't go to Tennessee; they play slow-down ball and it won't prepare you for the pro's." That advice may have been valid during Coach Mears' early years at Tennessee but transition fast break was the style played during my college career and the years after. In fact, during my freshman year, the style was so up-tempo that it enabled me to average 30.1 points per game and our team to score 70 and 80 points per night.

It was not the Vol offense that slowed games down; it was the other team's offense. They would take one to two minutes to take a shot. Opposing coaches thought they could wear down Tennessee's 1-3-1-defense by holding the ball for shots. Adolph Rupp detested competing against the type of defense the Vols played and their disciplined offense. He was one of the coaches who consistently told recruits that Tennessee had two speeds: slow and slower. But he failed to mention to the recruits that Tennessee gave him the worst thrashing of his coaching career—87-59—in 1968; the Vols did not hold the ball much that night.

Coach Mears took a lot of criticism for his style of play, but actually he was ahead of his time. Almost every team in America played a two-guard front but Tennessee played with one guard only. When you watch teams play today, observe how many have one-guard fronts—almost all of them.

Also, Coach was notorious for the Tennessee defensive scheme; however, Coach Aberdeen designed the defensive game plans. Being responsible for the Vol offensive strategy, Coach Mears required two and one-half hours of practice time compared to one hour on defense. The slow-down accusation of Coach Mears' program by his opponents was unjustified. As a matter of fact, over the years rival teams have successfully utilized his unique offensive tactics, even the teams who accused him of disciplined strategy.

Take a Stick to It

In 1972 the Volunteers traveled to Texas, for a game with Guy Lewis's Houston Cougars. The Cougars had an outstanding basketball team with a front-line of 6'7", 6'8", and 6'9". Their arena seated 13,000 fans and was filled to capacity.

Guy Lewis's teams had gained national notoriety through the years and in the late 1960's had challenged the UCLA Bruins for the number-one ranking. In fact, they ended the Bruins' long winning streak in a highly publicized game in the Houston Astrodome which featured a match-up between Lew Alcinder (Kareem Abdul Jabar) and Elvin Hayes.

In 1972 the renowned Cougars were eager to feast on the undermanned Volunteers. As the Vols warmed up for the game, displaying their Globetrotter maneuvers, they felt the crowd's intense focus upon them. That quickly changed when at the far end of the arena a circus cage inhabited by a live cougar was rolled onto the playing surface. As the animal was paraded, the crowd roared. The cage was placed behind our basket and an attendant stood guard with a long stick.

Wild animals, usually restless and voracious, tend to make me nervous, even caged ones. Now I've seen wild animals at football games in stadiums, but this was the first one I ever saw in a basketball arena. Compared to the Houston team, our physique was not very impressive, and if that Cougar escaped he would be looking at mostly appetizers at out end of the floor.

The attendant holding the stick created havoc. Every time he wanted the wild creature to roar he banged the cage. During the game Coach Aberdeen got up to prowl the sidelines. If he had been aware that the cougar's eyes focused on his every sideline move, "Beef" would have remained seated on the bench. We played Houston tough that night, losing by only a couple of points. I was most fortunate to have scored twenty-nine points in the game; however, if we had won, I would have probably been the first in the cage.

Coaches' Clinic

When the Vols played in the NIT in 1969, a wealth of coaching talent was present. Bob Knight, the Vols' opposing coach, was head coach at West Point. Don Devoe, who later coached the Vols, was his assistant. The Cadets' point guard was destined for future coaching greatness and his name was Mike Krzyzewski later known to Duke fans as "Coach K." And, of course, the Vols had Ray Mears who at the time was ranked near the top nationally in active coaching with a winning percentage of over seventy percent.

They Looked Good

Today's basketball players, placing great emphasis on their uniforms especially their shoes, philosophize that: "I've got to look good before I can show you what I've got." During Coach Mears' time there were only two choices when selecting athletic shoes: Chuck Taylor Converse high tops or low cuts. If you chose the low cuts, ankle wraps or taping was required. The shoes were available in only white or black. The Vols always wore white shoes except for one year during Ernie Grunfield's career when the team wore powder blue. The two most impressive characteristics of the Chuck Taylor shoes were that they cost $9.95 and would not show wear.

In the latter sixties, companies started to experiment with leather shoes and Mears liked experiments. He prided himself to be the first to try anything. Adidas manufactured a shoe that was white with orange stripes on the sides. It was an impressive looking shoe that enhanced the Vol uniform. Coach Mears ordered an ample supply of Adidas from John Cook at the Athletic House, and the Vols were on their way to becoming trendsetters. The Chuck Taylor shoes could take the punishment of daily practice; and the stylish leathers, still in the experimental stage, were tested for endurance only during games.

Games proved punishment enough for the Adidas shoes as player after player had problems. On occasion when a player made a cut to the basket this footwear had a tendency to tear, and several pairs of the Adidas did not survive the competitive rigors. The game of basketball has changed a lot through the years, but one thing has remained the same: Practice makes the player—not his shoes.

Where Have All the Shooters Gone?

When I watch college basketball today, I wonder where the outside shooters have gone. The players are bigger and stronger with more athleticism, but the outside shooting percentages have dropped drastically. While watching a game last year, I heard the announcer remark: "What a great outside shooter this kid is; he's hitting 37 percent on 3-point shots." Under Coach Mears, 37 percent from the perimeter would have landed you on the bench.

Today's coaches have stressed weight training to the extent that it has affected most players' release of the ball. With his arm appearing tight when the ball is released, the player does not have near the range he once had. I don't believe players work as much on shooting as they once did. Shooting is one aspect of basketball that you don't need assistance in practicing; all that is required is a ball and a basket. Today it seems that outdoor courts are more vacant than in times past and coaches open gyms for players to practice shooting and still no one shows. It seems that players are more interested in the flashy part of the game today— dunking the ball and offensive moves. Shooting is an art; there is nothing more beautiful than a player taking a long outside jump shot and the ball hitting nothing but the net. Tony Hinkle, the late coach of Butler University, put it best when asked which team would win the game. Tony's unprofound reply was: "The team that puts the ball through the goal the most is going to win."

Ray Mears' basketball teams had a lot of great scoring nights but none like the one they experienced at Georgia in 1973. On that night the Vols shot a sizzling 64 percent to scorch the Bulldogs 85-71. I don't believe any team in Vol basketball history has matched the wing position shooting that was exhibited in Athens that night. John Snow made 10 for 11 attempts, and I went 8 for 9 with most shots being from long range. The wings made 18 out of 20 attempted shots—for 90 percent. The Vols would have achieved a 90 percent shooting statistic as a team but a couple of our younger players, Rodney Woods and Len Kosmalski, needed a little more offensive practice. Woods went 7 for 15 and Kos, 7 for 17. Our other post player, Larry Robinson, was 4 for 4. So our two wings and Rob hit 91.6 percent in the game (22 for 24). In fact, there were only two Vols that missed more than one shot. Bill Seale was 1 for 1 and Lloyd Richardson 0 for 1. The impressed Georgia Coach Ken Rosemond remarked, "I can't remember seeing anything like that; I kept thinking our defense was doing pretty well but the Vol outside shooters kept pumping them in."

To be honest with you, Ken, I haven't seen anything like it again in my lifetime. Where have all the shooters gone?

Flying Glasses

During the Georgia game in Athens in 1973, Coach Mears came off the bench to protest an official's call. During the emotional act his eyeglasses sailed onto the playing floor. In the process of retrieving them, Coach Mears was assessed a technical foul by official Reggie Copeland who assumed the glasses were thrown onto the court in protest of his call. Mears pleaded his case by saying, "My glasses just fell off, and I've come onto the court to pick them up."

Years later, while reminiscing about the glasses incident, I decided to see if glasses could just fall off and end up ten feet from where I was sitting. I experimented with a loose pair and a snug pair. I jumped off the sofa, moved my head back and forth and up and down swiftly, stood on my head and rolled over on the floor trying to get the glasses off, but they stayed securely in place. I concluded a bad call by an official automatically made them pop off. I should have had my wife blow a whistle and signal a "T.

Roses for Excellence

Before a Southeastern Conference match up with Florida in Alligator Alley during the 1972 basketball campaign, Coach Mears presented each player a red rose. Analogous to the Kentucky Derby, he compared each team in the conference as "running for the roses." He emphasized the importance of reaching first place and striving to be number one. Benefiting from the motivational talk, the team shot 64.1 percent in the game to beat the Gators and former UT assistant coach, Tommy Bartlett. After the game Bartlett could only shake his head in response to the Vols' spectacular shooting performance. "Tennessee was unbelievable!" he remarked. The 64.1 percent followed the 64 percent shooting performance two nights earlier at Georgia.

The game was not decided by a starter's outside jumper but by a native Kentuckian who had spent most of his career in a reserve role; that player's name was Eddie Voelker. With eleven seconds to go, Eddie stole the ball from Florida guard Chip Williams and scored the winning basket. It was the only shot Eddie attempted during the entire game. A run for the roses, the Kentucky Derby and a Kentuckian hitting a last-second shot to win a game provided another exciting moment during the Ray Mears era in Big Orange Country.

Always Carry a New Pencil

 Having lost a crucial home game the previous night to Vanderbilt, I was on my way to class when I ran into Sam Venerable, the Head of the Physical Education Department. A great person, he was as honest as they come.

Sam, working at the scorer's table, had noticed during the Vanderbilt game that I had made some disapproving gestures regarding one of the official's calls. According to the popular P.E. Department Head, I was not exhibiting good sportsmanship conduct. I proceeded to tell him that I thought the officials made several bad calls that night destroying our chances of winning. I probably should not have made my feelings known to Sam; when the words came out I wished I could have retrieved them because I knew I was in for a reprimand.

Sam asked to see the pencil I was carrying to class. As I took it out of my notebook and handed it to him, he said, "By the looks of that eraser it appears you have made a few mistakes yourself."

Let's Purchase Alligator Alley

 Coach Mears used to enjoy making a spectacle of his outside sharpshooters. On one occasion while the Vols were having organized shooting practice in the Florida gym, several Gator student hecklers made an appearance.

Coach Mears had the outside marksmen count off the shots they made from the wing position, and at one point the players were up to twenty in a row. The hecklers, appalled by the outstanding shooting exposition, became quiet. Where upon Coach remarked, "Let's just buy this place with ten more in a row."

Hot Chocolate Time

When it came to psychology Coach Mears was way ahead of everybody else. He could read the minds of opposing coaches, officials, fans, and his own players. One day in practice I was performing poorly; nothing seemed to be going right.

I was not shooting well; I was making inaccurate passing decisions; and my defense was absent. What made it worse, Coach Aberdeen was "in my face" constantly. Aberdeen could turn your bad day into a death wish.

Coach Mears was aware I routinely drove to Maryville to see my fiancée nightly after practice. From time to time he would kid me by saying, "Edwards, did you go to Maryville last night to get hot chocolate?" Most of the time I would not answer him, but at this particular practice session I tried to out-psych him. Noticing that things were not going well for me, he halted practice and disgustingly asked: "Edwards, did you go to Maryville last night for hot chocolate?" I did not want to think a trip to Maryville to see my girlfriend had affected my performance this practice day so I retorted: "No, Coach, I didn't." Coach Mears then looked at me and said, "You should have; you are stinking this place up."

Movie Reruns

 Sitting in on a Coach Mears meeting before practice could be a humbling experience. Coach's mood set the tone for the thirty-minute meeting and the practice that followed. If a player was in the "doghouse," he could expect to be the subject for the day.

Mears could verbally chastise an anonymous player, but everybody in the room knew exactly about whom he was speaking. Following the meeting and on their way to the practice floor, players often made sarcastic remarks to the "poor soul" such as: "Your butt is grass today" or "Don't worry about it; it'll be someone else tomorrow." Coach's negative approach usually proved to have a positive result as the criticized player would give a good effort in practice that day.

Coach Mears routinely showed 8 mm game films in the meeting room, especially after a loss. He zeroed in on one play that he decided cost the team the win which did not necessarily occur in the last minutes of the contest. For instance, a player might have missed a crucial shot, but Coach would focus in on a loose ball or a rebound that was lost or maybe a lack of effort on a play that happened earlier in the game. Effort was everything to Coach. If you were twelve to fourteen points down and the game was all but over, you better still be diving for loose balls or the next week's practice sessions might be more than you could handle.

In the meeting room after a game we had lost, Coach emphasized that Len Kosmalski had not made an effort to retrieve a rebound that was crucial. The film portrayed the ball bouncing three times on the rim while Big Kos bounced three times, moving his upper body with his feet glued to the floor. Mears replayed the sequence at least twenty times remarking, "Look at this; I can't believe it; the ball bounces on the rim three times, and, Kos, the only thing you move are your head and shoulders all three times. I've never seen anything like it. Kos, what are you doing? It looks like you're watching a spaceship go up; look at your head." While talking, Coach moved the picture back and forth with the switch on the projector.

Big Kos had a super practice that day that, no doubt, helped prepare him for future SEC recognition.

Choosing a Leader

Coach Mears was an avid student of military history. While perusing the biographies of many battle-worn generals, he came to discover what made them such outstanding leaders and incorporated many of their strategies into his basketball program.

Boys grew up fast under the Mears system. Strict discipline, loyalty, maximum effort, cooperation, team concept and a respect for authority were hallmarks of the Vol program. Most players adjusted to the rigorous system while others could not adapt to the strict discipline and transferred to other schools. The team persevering in Coach Mears' program learned a valuable lesson in life—how to deal with adversity and accept defeat. Striving to become number one, every player was proud to be a student athlete at the University of Tennessee.

There was one Vol whom Coach Mears relied upon heavily—the captain. The captain, chosen by the squad, was the one that Coach confided in to get a feel from a player's perspective on methods to improve the program. The captain had to possess leadership qualities and the respect of his teammates; he was the number one player in the Mears system and the glue that held the team together.

The captain also enjoyed special privileges, such as having his own individual dressing stall in the locker room that was painted a different color from the other players' stalls. He sat in an orange chair in the meeting room that was placed in the number one spot while the other chairs were white. The captain acted as a team spokesman, making several speaking engagements to civic organizations, and was responsible for promoting the Big Orange Program. Being team captain was the highest honor bestowed on a Vol player.

Coach Mears always elected the team captain on a day of great military significance. It could have been a day a battle took place during the Civil War or World War II; regardless, he made it perfectly clear that picking the captain was one of the most important days in the Tennessee basketball program. The captain would take his team into battle, and all the outcomes would rest on his shoulders. The captain's dressing stall contained a list of all previous captains with their team's season records underneath.

In 1972 the Tennessee basketball program made history. The team elected Larry Robinson as the first African American basketball captain, and what a great leader Larry made. He was respected by all the players and coaches and was loved by the Tennessee fans. A transfer from Ferrum Junior College, he became an asset to the UT basketball program. Although he was not really vocal, he provided tremendous leadership in his efforts on the court.

To prove what an extraordinary athlete Larry was: Even though he had limited football experience, the Dallas Cowboys drafted him; and he played several seasons in the NFL. A marvelous team leader, Larry Robinson's tenure provided another vital chapter in Tennessee basketball history.

Can't—I Don't Know the Meaning

 When Coach Mears arrived on the Tennessee campus, he began to upgrade the basketball facilities. One of his priorities was to improve the locker room. He wanted to create a locker room that was comparable to Hollywood standards with each player treated as a star.

When Coach went to Athletic Director Bob Woodruff requesting the money for the project, Woodruff told him the following: "I can't provide the funds; they are not available." When Coach Mears heard the word *can't,* he knew the locker room would become a goal because *can't* was not a word used around the young coach. He went to the newly formed Orange Tie Booster Club, informing them of the importance of a quality locker and meeting room. Just about as fast as Bob Woodruff said, "Can't," contractors were framing the individual player's stalls and painters were coating the walls with fresh orange and white paint. Orange carpet was laid and motivational sayings were hung on the walls to inspire the players.

Rumor had it that while the work was in progress, Woodruff made an unscheduled inspection and was not happy with the unapproved remodeling. He wanted to know where the money came from and who approved the work. Regardless, Coach Mears had a number one basketball locker room and meeting room that he could use to entice recruits to his program. Coach always said that players did not have to belong to a fraternity because the basketball team served as your fraternity; the locker room became another place for the "basketball family" to gather when celebrating victories or agonizing a defeat. The room, a place of tremendous pride, became a highlight for friends and family while touring the campus.

During the remodeling process Coach Mears installed a stereo system for the purpose of furthering his theme of comparing our athletic contest to a Roman Gladiator battle. While players put on their uniforms, they were inspired by soundtracks from movies such as *Man from La Mancha, The Bridge Over River Kwai* and *Patton.* Emphasizing preparation for the fight, Coach remarked: "Boys, you're going into the arena for battle; you're either going to come out alive in glorious triumph or you're going to be carried out on your shield—dead." He felt if every player believed that strongly about the task at hand there were not going to be many losses. And he was right—not many Volunteer basketball teams during the Ray Mears tenure were carried out of the arena on their shields.

The reality of Coach Mears' remodeled University of Tennessee basketball locker room illustrated that the word *can't* never moved anyone to the top!

A Big Heart Inside the Orange

There is a saying, "You can never keep a good man down," and Coach Stu Aberdeen was such a man. In the fall of 1969 doctors at the University of Tennessee Hospital told the fiery Volunteer mentor that he would be unable to coach from the bench during the year because of a heart disorder; Coach would be allowed to practice the team but was prohibited from attending games. This diagnosis was like telling a top gun fighter pilot that he would have to spend a year in a flight simulator.

Coach Aberdeen inherited his heart condition. Rumor had it that one doctor had told him he had the heart of a sixty-year-old; and since coach was only in his latter thirties, this condition posed a serious health threat. It was assumed that Coach Aberdeen checked into the Med Center under an alias so that his condition would not jeopardize his chances of obtaining a future head coaching position. Regardless, Coach Aberdeen had a bad heart and he was in a profession that required a good "ticker," especially when most of the Vol games went "to the wire."

Coach's condition was kept extremely quiet and the 1969-70 season was the only one he sat out. What made Aberdeen's heart ailment so incredible was that he was so physically small and probably had less than ten percent body fat. He always took care of himself, eating low-fat foods and drinking skimmed milk.

During the entire season Coach Aberdeen pleaded with doctors for permission to coach on game nights but they adamantly refused. Not being on the floor with the rest of the Volunteers tore the insides out of the dedicated Coach. However, on at least one occasion and possibly more he arrived at a solution to the problem.

One of the colorful pre-game acts of the Mears Era "circus" included a gigantic orange parading around the floor. The enormous fruit was constructed of wood and chicken wire wrapped in paper and painted orange. The object required a couple of people standing inside to parade it around the floor. There were small holes in the gigantic mascot so that the individuals inside could peek out. Rumor had it that on several game nights Coach Aberdeen, taking his place inside the orange, had it directed to mid court so he could watch the Volunteers play.

As restless as Coach Aberdeen was on the bench, it is amazing that the orange was able to contain him, but it did. Although Coach Aberdeen's physical heart was defective, he possessed the emotional "heart" of a true champion and it never functioned more effectively than the nights he spent in the big orange, giving all the support he could to the Volunteer program.

Birth of the "Big Orange"

It is hard to imagine what Tennessee athletics would have been like without the influence of Ray Mears. On crisp fall Saturdays we watch 107,000 orange-clad fans cheer their beloved Vols at Neyland Stadium. During the heart of winter another 15,000-16,000 fans enter Thompson Boling Arena to cheer on the basketball Vols. Orange can be seen everywhere; in fact, a Tennessee fan not clad in orange was looked at as some kind of rare species.

When Coach Mears first came to the University of Tennessee, fans attended games clad in sports coats and ties; there was very little orange to be seen except on the uniforms of the Volunteers. That all changed when Ray Mears came back from a basketball recruiting trip in his home state of Ohio.

On that trip a lighted sign changed the face of Tennessee sports forever. Earlier in the evening Coach Mears had watched a high school player perform and was on his way back to the airport when he spotted a lighted advertisement which read: "Welcome to Marlboro Country." Within seconds he saw a different sign in his mind which read; "Welcome to Big Orange Country."

It did not take long for the color orange to become prominent in the Mears basketball program. The color could be seen everywhere— in buildings and bridges, on orange clad fans and on vehicles; even Gatorade turned to Vol-ade. Coach Mears had transformed the school colors into a statewide obsession. Some fans, when referring to the Tennessee Volunteers, would simply ask: "How's the 'Orange' going to do this weekend?" "Big Orange Country" was plastered on everything from stadium lights to car decals. When an out-of-state fan watching a Vol football game for the first time remarked, "I've never seen so much orange in my whole life," he knows where he is.

Coach Ray Mears initiated the 'Big Orange Theme"; he promoted it, was loyal to it and he won with it. On recruiting trips he always wore an orange blazer. When he came to Greenfield, Indiana, on a cold wintry Hoosier night in 1969 to watch me play a high school game, everyone in the gym knew what university he represented. There were other college coaches in attendance that night, but the fans were unaware of them. They knew Ray Mears was there because he was the only one wearing orange in the middle of winter among a crowd of four thousand.

A lot has changed since Ray Mears put the orange in the stands with his promotional genius. The power "T" is used in football now. Decals and sports apparel displaying "Big Orange Country" are less frequently seen these days. The large highway billboards in the state of Tennessee displaying the words: "This is big orange country" are mere memories. Over time, the word *country* has been deleted; however, *big orange* is bigger and stronger than ever. And to think it all had its roots on a midnight drive in Ohio!

Pins

Coach Mears loved motivational pins. He often returned from a coaches' clinic or corporate seminar with some type of pin he could use to motivate his players. He would have it duplicated for each of the team members to wear on their orange blazers. There were times that the players had so many pins on their blazer lapels that they looked like they had been presented a military award for courageous service. The logo on the motivational pins also eventually appeared on signs in the locker rooms and on the backs of the players' practice jerseys.

One of the motivational sayings that Coach Mears utilized can be seen today on football jerseys sold in stores. The front of the jerseys display a "XL." This insignia was first given to the Vol basketballers in pin form. A lot of people thought the letters stood for *extra large* but this assumption was untrue. Saying the letters *XL* quickly sounds like the word *excel*. While playing at Tennessee I must have explained this to people a thousand times. Fans would take one look at my practice jersey with the huge white XL letters on the back and remark: "You don't look to be extra large," or "Does the basketball program have any other jerseys that are not extra large?" Then I would have to look at the fan and reply, "Say XL quickly."

Another pin we had was the triple A bar zero. Coach got this idea from General George Patton who initiated the motivational insignia during World War II and attached it to the entrance of his ranch in Texas. It translated to the following: "We can win any time, any place, any how, bar none." I like this pin because there is no way the average person could ever figure it out. I usually let most of the people try to guess its significance but eventually told them what it meant.

The pin that was a great mystery to fans was the ZD emblem. The best guess I ever heard was that it meant zone defense. Since we played zone defense the majority of the time the guess made sense. But in truth, ZD stood for zero defects. That meant the team that made the fewest mistakes would win the game. How true this was during the Mears era. If our basketball team made more than ten errors in a game, we usually lost. There were many games in which we made six or fewer mistakes during the forty minutes of play. Mears' teams were trained not to make blunders, and the zero defect label was a constant reminder on what the success of the program depended.

Every once in a while I will get one of these pins out and attached it to my coat lapel and just for old times sake I will begin to answer people's questions as to what it means. It brings back a lot of old memories and on some days memories are what makes life tolerable.

Family Plane Trips and Male Hormones

Away games and plane trips were special times for the Tennessee basketball family. The early Mears' Era airplane was named "The General," and in later years flights were chartered. The trips were a time for the Volunteers to come together as players ate meals together, practiced together, roomed together and entertained one another by playing cards or telling jokes. The team came to be a close unit on these trips; and if we won the road games, we even became a more tightly knit group.

The plane carried an array of big orange supporters. There was the coaching staff— Ray Mears, Stu Aberdeen, A.W. Davis, Gerald Oliver, and in earlier years Tommy Bartlett and Sid Hatfield. Marvin West and Ben Byrd were regulars from the local newspapers. F. M. Williams represented the sportswriters from Nashville. Haywood Harris and Bud Ford were aboard to cover the game for the Sports Information Department at UT. John Ward, voice of the Vols, was along as was athletic trainer Tom Wall and head manager David Mills. Reverend James Tipton, who had played football at Penn State for Joe Paterno, was an important part of the group. The Big Orange Tie Club was also well represented with Ken Rice, Creed Daniels, Harry Bettis, among others to show their support.

I can still vision Ken Rice in his overcoat and tie waiting to board the plane with his orange travel bag draped across his shoulder, going from one player to another wishing them the best of luck and always asking about one's family. Plane trips were always a special time for Volunteer players and provided fond memories for all of us, especially for players who had never flown before. Upon boarding the plane squad members were presented a box lunch catered by Regas Restaurant that consisted of a cold-cut sandwich, chips, and a drink. Sportswriter Marvin West, as an enticement for a possible scoop, passed out candy bars.

On some flights if the weather was calm and stars were shining brightly, the pilots would permit a player or two to enter the cockpit. Entering the cockpit made me a little uncomfortable as I viewed the sophisticated instrument panel that could malfunction.

Every chartered plane trip carried one stewardess. One stewardess and a plane full of twenty-four varsity and freshmen Volunteer basketballers were overwhelming odds for a female flight attendant. There were always a couple of Volunteers who made a rivalry out of who could show the stewardess the most attention. These few players always seemed to use the same routine on every flight since the stewardess was never the same. They would wait for the inside cabin lights to go off and then they would move toward the back of the plane away from the coaching staff that was seated up front. Then the action would begin. The Volunteer flight would be transformed into "the love plane."

One player would raise his hands as if to request a coke or peanuts and when the stewardess approached him he would reply with a whisper so she could not understand what he wanted. Then he would ask her to bend over if she could not hear and then he would whisper more softly. He kept whispering softer until he got her closer to him and then he would kiss her on the cheek. Usually the stewardess would be quite taken aback by this action, but the player had accomplished his mission. I kept waiting for one of those stewardesses to give the player a good right palm, but he must have made a pretty good impression because she usually responded with a warm smile.

Another "contestant" would work his way to the back of the plane and leave a vacant seat to his side. He would then entice the flight attendant to sit next to him, and as they talked he would move closer and closer. The next thing you knew the attendant would be on his lap and he would be caressing her shoulders. This action put an end to the mission, as the attendant would abruptly arise and explain she could not behave in this manner while on her job.

Another "love plane" game involved two participants. One player would talk to the stewardess and get her to lean over while another player across the aisle would caress her lower legs. Usually this would be the end of the game on that particular flight because the stewardess would head to the front of the plane to never be seen in the back again, regardless of any requests.

On the "UT Basketball Love Plane" for some Vols, male hormones prevailed over common sense.

The Voice

During the Mears years one individual that had a huge part in promoting Coach's program was the Voice of the Vols, John Ward. Ward may have been the best play-by-play radio announcer in America in his day. He not only announced games, he painted a picture. The action was described so vividly that listeners felt as though they were actually watching the game, rather than just listening to it; few radio play-by-play sports commentators have the ability to describe the actions in such a spectacular manner.

Ward brought Big Orange basketball to thousands of Tennesseans who were unable to purchase one of the 12,700 tickets for a game in Stokely. He made phrases such as, "It's basketball time in Tennessee" and "Bottom!" a part of UT basketball lore. Ward's expressions became a part of many youngsters' vocabulary. Vol players during games did not just take long shots when John Ward was announcing; they took shots from downtown Maryville or Clinton. Sometimes shots that went through the goal exploded in his description. For example, "Rodney Woods takes a long jumper from downtown Knoxville—bang!" John would holler. As a shot went through the goal, you could hear the roar of the crowd in the background on the radio. John Ward's outstanding commentary was responsible for making basketball legends out of UT players. Vols became bigger than life due to the voice of one man.

Sometimes John would even "officiate" a game. "You walked, Robey," he would say, or "King is fouled inside—no call." John was "big orange" through and through; after every game it was obvious he had given one hundred percent because he could be seen with a towel wrapped around his neck as he left the arena.

John Ward, who earned the respect of all the players, gave the impression to the Vol basketball players that he was a quiet and somewhat reserved individual. In my four years at Tennessee I can never recall sitting down and carrying on a conversation with him, as his demeanor appeared to be that of a private individual.

On occasion when I returned to my hometown where Tennessee basketball games were aired and folks asked questions regarding John Ward, I could not answer many. John made the listener feel so much at ease and such a part of the program that many felt they actually knew him personally. The Voice of the Vols, possessing a knack in creating "household" terms, promoted the UT basketball team and individual players like no other announcer ever had. Ray Mears took his basketball teams to the top of the SEC, and he could not have had a better promotional man than John Ward.

However, I will remember the Vol commentator more for what he did not say than what he did say. When our paths crossed, he would always stretch his right arm upward and drop his hand toward the floor as if to signal "Bottom!" Without saying a word his body language was gesturing me to "bomb" them in. That's the John Ward I'll always remember.

You Better Run

Coach Mears described Howard Bayne, the outstanding post player that played for him in the early sixties, as follows: "He was the most fierce rebounder that ever put on an orange and white uniform; he had a mean streak that struck fear in opposing players." Howard's aggressive nature peaked during a game against the University of Florida when the opposing Gator center began to physically intimidate Howard; the powerful centers exchanged words, elbows, and shoves.

As each team headed to the opposite end of the court on a fast break, big Howard had taken all he could from the Florida strong man. Howard, giving him a good shot to the upper chops, sent the muscular Gator reeling. The wounded player retreated to the stands in an attempt to escape big Howard's wrath, but the fierce Vol followed in hot pursuit, grabbing the Gator and giving him precisely what he deserved. Howard won the skirmish in a first round knockout.

All I Want to Do Is Shoot

 Howard Bayne was upset with Coach during his career because he was limited to the number of shots he was allowed to attempt in a game. In fact, the whole team was prohibited from shooting a lot in those early days of the Mears Era due to the disciplined offensive style.

Unfortunately, big Howard had signed on with the Vols to become part of the Mears star system, meaning players were recruited to perform certain duties according to their abilities. Some players were shooters, some ball handlers and others rebounders. Howard had one of the most grueling and unappreciated jobs in the system—rebounding. Performing his assignment with excellence, Howard became one of the greatest rebounders that ever played on the "hill." However, during his playing days he wanted more; he wanted to shoot.

In a game against Kentucky Coach Mears had his team in an extra slow mode against the more talented Wildcats; in fact, Howard said that both teams were hardly moving and it was the quietest crowd before whom he had ever performed. The opposing center was Cotton Nash, Kentucky's All-American. Since the game was so slow and each Vol trip to their offensive end was a demonstration in dribbling and passing, big Howard and Cotton would merely stand at the free throw line with arms folded and converse. Cotton said, "Bayne, are we going to play tonight? I dressed out to play basketball, and here we stand." Big Howard responded, "I'm with you, Cotton. I've been asking Mears to shoot more for years, but I've been hired as a rebounder; and since we're not taking shots, I'm not working tonight."

He's Not a Marlboro Man

In Bernard King's first Kentucky game at Lexington, the Vols suffered a heart-breaking three-point loss. As the team was leaving the court, a Kentucky fan that lacked good judgment tossed a lighted cigarette that hit Bernard in the face. The All-American who had endured enough hard knocks in his short lifetime, pursued the fan. Just when the Kentucky Bluegrasser wished he had never smoked a cigarette, Coach Aberdeen intervened and pulled Bernard away.

In the locker room sportswriters who had witnessed the incident began chastising the Vol center for his conduct. Taking all the verbal abuse he could from them, Bernard arose from a bench, went to one of the sportswriters, looked him in the eye, took his forefinger and planted it deliberately on the writer's chest and made a prediction: "As long as I'm at Tennessee I'll never lose to Kentucky again, and you can print it."

The rest is Tennessee basketball history. The Vols beat the Cats the next five games. No other Vol basketball team ever beat Kentucky five consecutive games and to think the streak began with a lighted cigarette.

The Player Coach

During Coach Mears' tenure at Tennessee it was obvious that he treated some players differently than others. The captain of the team was one such player who shared a special relationship with Coach. Bill Justus, a former captain went a step farther in his assessment of Mears' relationship with his players. He believed that Coach Mears treated all his players as kids except one and that individual was captain Ron Widby whom he placed on a pedestal. Bill would say, "Coach Mears treated Ron like he was a member of the coaching staff. I don't know why, but all of us were just kids and Ron for some reason was on the Coach's level."

I recently asked Coach Mears about this assessment. Grinning from ear to ear, the former Vol mentor gave me the impression that Bill had been right. Coach remarked, "Ron Widby was the greatest all-around player that ever played for me; he could do it all. He was a great outside shooter, a great passer, and a fierce competitor; he was very knowledgeable on the floor and a great team leader. Ron was the best captain I ever had and the best athlete. You know, he played football also."

Well, Bill, you were right. I know of no other Vol basketballer that played for Coach that met the aforementioned criteria. We were all "just kids" when compared to Ron.

First Year Gems

During the first year of Ray Mears' tenure at the University of Tennessee he coached two All-Americans—A. W. Davis and Danny Schultz. According to Coach, A. W. was the first truly outstanding post player to wear the orange uniform; and Schultz, a byproduct of Hiwassee Junior College, was his first prolific long-range shooter.

What a way to start a major college coaching career!

Mister Loyalty

To the players, he was known as Mr. Rice. To Coach Mears, he became one of his most devoted UT basketball supporters and a close personal friend. The number one characteristic that Coach valued in an individual was loyalty, and Ken Rice definitely fit that bill. Ken attended most practice sessions and made every road trip. He was continuously seeking ways to assist Coach Mears in his program. Originally from a small town in Indiana, a state that tends to produce devoted basketball fans, Ken loved the game.

Ken, owner of a successful car dealership in Knoxville, accompanied Coach Mears on some of his recruiting trips. When Coach wore his orange blazer, so did Mr. Rice. During Mears' tenure, Ken was the only loyal supporter I can remember who ever occupied the team bench. At some away games, Mr. Rice would position himself at the end of the bench next to the Vol-ade container. This location gave him sufficient time to dodge flying clipboards, towels, cups and occasionally Coach Aberdeen. At times Joe Dean, the television commentator for SEC games, would announce: "Coach Ken Rice is sitting on the Vol bench." Ken, offering encouragement to all the players, always greeted them with a smile and a handshake. At the conclusion of their career many Vol basketballers, showing their appreciation to Mr. Rice, purchased vehicles from his dealership.

A portion of the tremendous success experienced during the Ray Mears Era could be attributed to Mr. Ken Rice's devotion to the Big Orange Basketball Program.

Take Your Money and Leave...
Forever

In 1973 the basketball Vols were scheduled to play Temple University in the finals of the Volunteer Classic. The Classic, a tournament of pride for Coach Mears, had become one of the premier Christmas tourneys in America. Each year he invited outstanding teams to Knoxville from each section of the country. Some of the former teams that performed in the classic were Michigan State, Providence, Syracuse and Missouri.

On a cold December night, the unexpected occurred. The game began as planned by the Vols as they obtained the tip and scored the first two points. Then boredom set in. Temple, bringing the ball to their offensive end of the court, looked at Tennessee's standard 1-3-1-zone defense and proceeded to hold the ball while attempting to divert the Vols into a man-to-man defense. The Owl coach obviously was unaware of Coach Mears' philosophy as hell would have to freeze over before Coach would exit his zone defense. Staring at each other at half court, each squad dared the other to make a move. The 12,700 fans became restless and voiced their disapproval. The integrity of the Classic was in jeopardy as even the two game officials were obviously perplexed. The half time score was 2-0, and the nightmare ended with a score of 11-6 in the Vols favor.

After the game Coach Mears cornered the Temple coach and said, "We paid you $10,000 to come in here, play basketball and entertain the fans and you pull this. You will never be asked to come here again as long as I'm coach." Mears required his team to remain on the floor and scrimmage for an extra half hour, while the irate fans exited the arena

I'm not sure what the interest is on $10,000 in thirty years; but if UT ever schedules Temple University in Knoxville again, the Owls better bring a check.

Match Met

If there was an assistant basketball coach in America that worked players harder than Stu Aberdeen during the 1960's and '70's, I would like to have met him. Coach was the ultimate taskmaster. When asking Coach Mears about Stu Aberdeen, he responded by saying, "Stu Aberdeen was the greatest thing to happen to my program; he coached the defense and the big men; he was a tireless worker."

But when Bernard King arrived on the UT campus, Coach Aberdeen had met his match. In fact, it only required one practice. Bernard took the court that first day and reported to Coach Aberdeen for big-man drills. Fifteen minutes into the session, he walked to other end of the court where Coach Mears was drilling the guards and forwards on shooting. Bernard, tapping Mears on the shoulder, complained, "Coach, I'm not getting enough work down there." Coach Mears, thinking his prize recruit was attempting to evade the drills, then looked at Bernard and remarked, "Well, what do you want to do about it?" "I want to go over to a side goal and work on my own," the New Yorker replied. Believing that Bernard was going to take a rest from the intense workout at the opposite end of the court, Mears reluctantly agreed to his request.

What Coach Mears saw for the next forty-five minutes was the most amazing individual practice routine he had ever witnessed in all his years of coaching. "Bernard didn't quit moving for the entire forty-five minutes; he would shoot the ball and sprint after it, never stopping to catch his breath. He practiced offensive moves that Coach Aberdeen and I had never seen. Bernard had watched and studied pro players and then made their moves a part of his game. I never saw any player work this hard in all my years of coaching," Mears recalled.

Continuing, Mears stated, "From that day until the end of his career I let him work on his own. It was the best decision I ever made because Bernard became one of the most prolific scorers in UT basketball history."

The Toughest Loss

During the "Ernie and Bernie Show" era at UT Coach Mears suffered his toughest loss. The game in 1977 was against Syracuse during the NCAA Tournament in what Mears termed a "survival" game. The Vols possessed the potential to have advanced in the "big dance." He had two All-Americans in Bernard King and Ernie Grunfeld. He also had another player, Mike Jackson, who quite possibly could have attained higher recognition in those years but was overshadowed by the Ernie and Bernie accolades.

The Syracuse game had been close all the way; but with six minutes remaining, UT's hopes were diminished as Bernard King fouled out. The New Yorker was whistled for an offensive charge, which Coach disputes to this day: "Bernard had such great body control that he seldom ran over anyone. Most of his fouls were defensive."

The Vols battled to overtime, but again adversity struck. Ernie Grunfeld attained his fifth personal foul and with the two UT All-Americans occupying the bench, Syracuse was victorious. For Coach Mears it was his most devastating loss. Vol fans cannot help but think what might have been if King and Grunfeld had not fouled out. Would this team have been the first UT Men's Basketball Squad to become NCAA champions?

Help from the Gridiron Boys

One of the biggest wins during the Mears Era occurred when the Tennessee boys beat Adolph Rupp and his fabled Rupp's "Runts" in the old armory during the final game of the season for both teams. Entering the contest undefeated, Kentucky later went to the finals of the NCAA Tournament in 1966 before losing to Texas Western University.

Prior to that storied night in Knoxville, the Cats had never played before such a hostile crowd. The old armory was packed as usual as the Tennessee football players decided they would make the night just a little more miserable for the "Baron of the Bluegrass."

All-American quarterback Dewey Warren, known as the Swamp Rat, organized the gridiron entourage and conveniently arranged for the entire squad to sit directly behind Adolph Rupp. Throughout the game the football team verbally disrupted Rupp who was not easily intimidated; however, on this night the football team frustrated him to the extent that his Cats fell so far behind they could never recover.

At the game's conclusion a shining moment transpired in Tennessee Basketball history. The football players rushed the court and hoisted the basketball team on their shoulders. Jimmy Cornwall, a Vol guard who had an incredible game, was lifted to the goal so he could cut down the net. According to Coach Mears, this event marked the first and only time the football squad ever carried a UT basketball team off the court. The quarterback of a football team is its number one leader, and Dewey Warren proved what kind of leader he was on the night Ray Mears and his Vols beat Rupp's Runts to spoil their perfect record for the season.

The Most Unbelievable Shot

Ray Mears and his crew of Volunteers were attempting to make it five straight over Joe Hall and the Kentucky Wildcats. The game was in Lexington, and the Vols' hopes for a win were diminishing fast as the Cats were up by ten late in the game. But the Tennessee squad fought hard, hitting several outside shots to close within two. As the clock was ticking down, Bernard King took a high lob pass from Vol wingman Austin Clark. Losing his balance with his body parallel to the floor, King put the ball into the basket. "It was the most unbelievable shot I ever saw; it showed everybody just what a great athlete and player Bernard King was," Coach Mears reminisced. The shot tied the game and the Vols won in overtime.

An autographed display of the shot hangs in Coach Mears' home and is a constant reminder of the night a miracle shot beat Kentucky.

The Twelve-Foot Goals

Coach Mears preferred his program to be different; he felt like being unique and out of the norm earned your program publicity. In the mid-1960's he stepped from the norm when he decided to raise the basketball goals to twelve feet and hold an intra-squad scrimmage to demonstrate how the height alteration would affect the game. *Sports Illustrated Magazine,* intrigued by the height adjustment, sent a writer to cover the game. The general consensus favored the ten-foot goals, but when Tommy Boerwinkle, the seven-foot Vol center, made his comment, the final decision was rendered. Big Tom stated, "It was hard for me to play on the twelve-foot goals."

Since Tommy was one of the tallest guys in America at the time, one can only imagine what a challenge twelve-foot goals would pose for other players.

The Uniform—A Tennessee Tradition

When Ray Mears came to the University of Tennessee, he discovered orange uniforms were as much a part of the basketball tradition as pinstripes are unique to the New York Yankees. Upon his arrival as head basketball coach of the UT Vols, Mears redesigned the team's uniforms.

The front of the jersey displayed a small number with the word *Tennessee* inscribed across the top and the word *Volunteers* underneath—a lot of letters to crowd on the front of a jersey. The back of the jersey exhibited a large number with the player's last name printed above. Coach Mears wanted people aware that Boerwinkle, Widby, Davis, Grunfield and King were Volunteers.

Home uniforms contained white with orange lettering outlined in pale blue while away uniforms were orange with white lettering outlined in pale blue. Each uniform was designed with a touch of class, a tradition of Coach Mears' program. In later years the pale blue outlining, not deemed a representation of "toughness," was replaced with black.

Teams that won a total of seventy percent of their games wore the Mears designed uniforms—another tradition in Tennessee basketball history.

You Didn't Look for the Dot

Before the start of the 1971-72 basketball campaign, I was approached by Ray Bussard, the UT Swim Coach. Coach Bussard, a lot like Coach Mears, combined hard work, discipline and showmanship to make his program one of the best in the country. He paraded his team wearing coonskin hats into the Aquatic Center as part of their pre-meet ritual. He even used college co-eds dressed in orange and white to report the scoring.

Watching a Coach Bussard swim meet was like watching the basketball Vols in water. Every swim meet was a spectacle. Coach Bussard, possessing some basketball knowledge, informed me that he could improve my free throw shooting ability. He remarked: "Mike, when you go to the free throw line there will be a small dot in the middle of the free throw stripe; this dot is on all gym floors where the seams join. Put your right foot in line with the dot and you are directly in front of the goal. Now you're ready to shoot."

That year when shooting a free throw, I always looked for the small dot and the alignment which improved my shooting average to eighty-six percent from the foul line. Every time I passed Coach Bussard in the dining hall he would ask, "Are you still looking for that dot?" To which I would reply, "Yes, I am." With a warm smile he would give me an encouraging pat on the back.

In the final game of the season against Kentucky for the Southeastern Conference Championship I missed a crucial free throw that could have tied the game. When passing Coach Bussard the following day, he grabbed my arm and said. "You didn't look for that dot last night; I watched you before you shot the free throw and you didn't look at the floor one time." Everyone thought the pressure of the situation was responsible for the miss, but I guess the real reason was I did not line up with the dot.

The Black Patch

As a youngster, I mowed Ken Orr's yard. I'll never forget those crisp, colorful fall Indiana Saturdays when I would head to his house, wearing a toboggan to keep my head warm and a Notre Dame sweatshirt to cover my shoulders. I was a huge Irish fan and would usually take a radio to listen to their football game while I worked. Mr. Orr paid me $2.50 to mow his yard—big money at the time for a young lad.

I never forgot Ken Orr when I headed for Knoxville and the University of Tennessee. I wrote him and his wife Thelma regularly, and it always made me happy to receive a letter from them. I always hoped he would be able to see me perform in college, but that dream never became a reality.

In the early summer of 1971 I brought my future wife Debbie on a trip to Indiana to visit my parents. Customarily, on trips home, I made a visit to the Orrs. On this trip I took Debbie along so she could meet Ken and Thelma. After a brief visit, Mr. Orr invited me to his garage, explaining he had something to show me. Upon entering the garage I discovered that Ken did not have anything to show me; he just wanted to talk in private. He wanted to express how proud he was of me and what a wonderful girl he thought Debbie was, stating," I think you ought to stick with her." He gave me some money so I could take her out to dinner and I thanked him.

Two years later Debbie and I were married. Little did I know that one week later after visiting with Mr. Orr he would be gone. One of my fondest memories is that he got to meet the girl I later married before he passed away. Ken was seventy-seven years old when he died.

During the 1971-72 basketball season at Tennessee, I wore a black patch stitched to my basketball uniform in Ken Orr's honor. Our team became Southeastern Conference co-champions that year. It was a phenomenal year for the Tennessee basketball family and a special year for me as I dedicated the season to my good friend Ken Orr.

T.N.T.

Coach had taken all the criticism he could handle from opposing coaches who were labeling the Vols as a slow-down program. So in 1973 he unveiled the T.N.T. attack. T.N.T. stood for Tennessee's Nuclear Tempered offense. Sounds sophisticated, doesn't it? The T.N.T. was so complicated that after thirty years I am still trying to figure out the concept. The coaching staff in a five-page promotional booklet compared the Tennessee offense to that of nuclear fusion. Are you lost yet? Here is a sampling:

"The three-D offense under extreme pressure required a cohesive nuclear force among the ball handler and the four players without the ball—or a nucleus. Thus emerged Tennessee's nuclear tempered offense. Still with me?

According to this nuclear theory each twenty minute half is a half-life. Once the timer starts the clock radio active disintegration occurs, inevitably with a gradual loss of energy by each team. The objective of the T.N.T. offense is to reduce the loss of energy or retain a meta stable state, that is, being able to maintain stability at a high energy level. The objective of the opposition is to reduce Tennessee to a ground state or the lowest energy level. Still there?

In order to discourage fission the offensive players strive to maintain proper symmetry. A balance among offensive positions prevents the defenders from two-timing the player having possession of the ball and also prevents the overplay of an outstanding offensive player. This spacing should allow high-percentage bombardment of the target area (the rim) which will produce "stars" (points) with more proficiency than any other team in the nation. Still awake?

Proton occupies a special position in the Vols scheme because the greatest contribution to the mass of the universe is made by protons. The hydrogen atom consists of the positive nucleus proton and there is an overwhelming cosmic abundance of hydrogen in the universe. The player who has possession of the ball at any time is designated "pro," an abbreviation of "proton."

When playing at Tennessee, I never pictured myself as being compared to a proton as opposing fans called us other names that were not as flattering. The T.N.T. went into high gear in 1973. No one really knew what it was but the letters were in orange so fans knew it had to be good. Protons, neutrons, fusion, fission, alpha decay and Tennessee basketball—I cannot believe the concept did not win a Nobel Prize.

Stu's Impersonator

Roger Peltz, the unicycle rider and juggler of three balls in the warm ups, was also the team comedian. He practiced extensively to impersonate famous people. He developed his talent to the degree that it was difficult to distinguish Roger's voice from the real person. One voice that he perfected was that of UT Assistant Coach Stu Aberdeen. "Rog," a daring guy, was not brave enough to imitate Stu's voice in his presence, perceiving that the consequences could possibly outweigh the enjoyment. Coach Aberdeen could run you on "suicides" forever, never tiring of the drill.

Although Roger was hesitant in joking with Coach Aberdeen, the other players were fair game. One night after observing a teammate's miserable performance in practice, Roger decided he would add to the player's problems. He went to the coaches' offices in the field house that were adjacent to Gibbs Hall to make sure Coach Aberdeen was working late, and, sure enough, the fiery coach was burning the midnight oil. Peltz, returning to his room, called the disgruntled player and said, "Hey, Big Guy, Coach Aberdeen here. Son, you're not putting out in practice—no guts. We have to have people here who work hard—gonna take you off scholarship. Come to my office immediately." The shocked player, leaving his dorm room with deep concern, passed Peltz who, with a straight face, asked him, 'Where're you going at this hour?" The player responded, "Maybe home."

When the player arrived at Coach Aberdeen's office, Stu was oblivious to what the distressed Vol was talking about when he asked, "When do I need to move out of the dorm?"

Where's the Home Court Advantage?

Stokely Athletic Center, home of the Vols, was an exciting place to play basketball with 12,700 fans in attendance. Through the years Tennessee did not lose many home games. However, compared to other SEC schools, Stokely Center did not provide UT players with the same home court advantages. In fact, players at UT used to jokingly compare the arena's atmosphere to that of an opera house or morgue as it was so quiet at times you could hear the ball bounce on the tartan surface. At Stokely when the opposing team was introduced, the Big Orange fans applauded; in fact, the only people the Vol fans booed were the officials. However, at away games Vol players could expect to be greeted with boos and flying objects hurled from the stands.

Coach Mears went through a period when the students were not happy with his style of play. The student newspaper, *The Daily Beacon,* made accusative comments that the Vols played for second position, which qualified them for the NIT. The paper convinced the student contingent that accelerated play would lead to more championships. The players read these articles and believed the insinuations were invalid. Coach Mears was one of the most competitive coaches in the country, and his extensive practice sessions were not designed for second place.

To voice their public displeasure of the Vols' disciplined style of play, many students began to boo Coach Mears and his staff before home games when they were introduced. Eventually the conduct of the disgruntled fans resulted in the PA announcer discontinuing the introduction of the coaching staff. However, this exhibition of displeasure had little effect on Coach Mears as his teams continued to win over seventy percent of their games, and students continued to pick up their allotment of tickets. The only real question at the time was: "Where's the home court advantage?"

Take the Charge, Boy

Coach Ray Mears invited Bob Knight to his UT Coaches Clinic in the fall of 1972. Coach Knight had just begun his tenure at Indiana University after a successful stint at West Point. His teams had the reputation of playing a discipline offense and a tenacious defense.

One part of his coaching presentation at the clinic demonstrated how to take an offensive charge. Coach Mears had arranged for his freshmen team to be present so that clinic coaches could use them in drills. Coach Knight put the players to work. He picked Denton Jones, a former outstanding player from Knoxville Central High School, to position himself under the goal, and he instructed 7'1" Len Kosmalski to drive into him.

When anticipating the inevitable Coach Mears should have been looking for a good life insurance salesman or at least put a call in to the UT emergency room because this match-up was doomed from the start. Denton, being a guard, stood a mere 6'1" and weighed probably 170 pounds; Kos, on the other hand, weighed in at well over 225 pounds—an obvious mismatch. The drill proceeded with big Kos dribbling directly into the hapless Jones, sending the prized guard end over end with his head striking the floor. Denton sustained a serious head injury and never fully recovered from the collision.

Later in the year he struck his head again during a freshman game against Kentucky. Doctors would not permit him to play at UT again for fear that another injury to the head might prove fatal. The accident was an unfortunate incident for a young man who had high hopes of playing for the Vols. At least Denton could boast that his basketball career was ended by one of the game's greatest coaches—Bob Knight.

You Are All Invited to Duke

 In 1972 the NCAA informed Coach Stu Aberdeen and the Tennessee basketball staff they could no longer run a preseason program with just scholarship players. Aberdeen, a step ahead of the system, developed the idea of calling the pre-season program a fitness class and allowing the student body to participate. The physical education department at UT was receptive to the idea, and the details of the class were posted in the *Daily Beacon*.

The first day of pre-season practice that year ten or so nonscholarship students were enrolled in the fitness class. A few of these students had long hair that Coach Aberdeen found offensive. Most of these fitness gurus were not in very good shape and at the end of the day they were barely able to stand up. Most of the walk-ons never made it through the first drills, and none lasted more than two days.

The way they exited the class was unique: usually they would hyperventilate and attempt to communicate with coaches through hand signals, gesturing they needed water. They would then crawl to the drinking fountain, attempting to get some liquid into their system. Some used the opportunity to throw up in one of Coach Aberdeen's puke buckets that were conveniently placed around the court. Next they would slowly sneak out the door never to return to the class again.

Paying the Price

Being from the eastern part of the United States, Steve Hirschorn had a great love for the game of basketball. When he enrolled at the University of Tennessee he decided to try out for the Volunteer Basketball Team. "Hirsch" made the squad. He lacked the skills of other players, but a competitive spirit compensated for his lack of talent. The small of stature, mediocre shooter had difficulty competing in the SEC. However, Steve was determined to make a contribution.

Coach Mears refused to offer him a scholarship, as he was a walk-on player, so Steve had to pay his own way to school. He practiced with the team, lived in the dorm and traveled to all the away games. For three years Hirsch paid the price in more ways than one. He earned the respect of his teammates but he wanted more; he wanted to play.

Approaching Coach Mears during his senior year, Hirsch expressed an unfulfilled and dissatisfied feeling regarding his status on the team. Subsequent to their conversation Mears remained skeptical of Steve's credentials; there were so many negatives outweighing the positives. However, when Eddie Voelker, the Vol point guard, began to struggle with his play, Coach Mears reassessed Steve's role on the team and gave him the opportunity to lead the Vol offense. Steve Hirschorn stepped into the point guard position and performed admirably. Even though he was instructed to limit his shooting attempts, he unselfishly passed the ball to the seven-foot center, Len Kosmalski, and other excellent shooters, that was essential for the success of the Vol offense.

Because of his hard work, dedication, and loyalty to the Vol Program during his senior year at UT, Steve Hirschorn was awarded a scholarship, and it was one of the best investments Coach Mears ever made. As a result of Hirsch's leadership, the Volunteers went on to win a SEC co-championship in 1972.

Legends of Cadiz

 Ray Mears' first coaching job was in Cadiz, Ohio, a town that boasted two renowned former citizens, Clark Gable and General George Custer. Throughout Mears' career a resemblance of both of these legends was manifested in coach's basketball personality.

Gable was "Mr. Hollywood," debonair, classy and the "toast of tinsel town." Mears was the master showman of the Tennessee Volunteers, always traveling first class with his team and the "toast of Knoxville." Custer, a Civil War hero, was confident and brash, believing he was invincible. A decision-maker that rolled the dice, Custer was feared and respected by foes. Coach Mears was the clever strategist, frequently out-foxing his opposition. Confident in his Vols, Mears won the respect of other SEC coaches and even challenged the Baron of the Bluegrass for coaching greatness.

Clark Gable, General George Custer, and Coach Ray Mears—all legends of Cadiz.

No Special Treatment for Wildcats

 When playing his archrival, Adolph Rupp and the Kentucky Wildcats, Coach Mears schemed to disrupt the Baron's game preparation. On arriving in Knoxville, the Cats requested a 5:30 p.m. practice time the day prior to the game.

This request seemed logical as Coach Mears' troops concluded their practice at 5 p.m., but the Vol mentor informed Adolph that 7 p.m. would be the earliest he could occupy the arena. Observers close to the Vol program said Mears did not want Rupp on the floor any earlier because he thought Kentucky might spy on the Vols, but Coach Mears vehemently denied the accusations. However, he never denied his cunning plan to rupture Adolph's schedule; he enjoyed provoking the Baron. One year Coach Rupp, so annoyed with the inconvenient practice plan, took his team to a nearby town to workout.

Rupp's strategy did not pay dividends, however, as his team was beaten by the Vols the following night.

Tartan

 Many fans believed that Coach Mears had been influential in the selection of the Tartan surface for the Tennessee basketball program. The Vol mentor used the Tartan rubber-playing surface as an asset when recruiting players. Emphasizing the surface to recruits, he took pride in the fact the Vols were the first to install such a court on campus.

In truth, Coach Mears was not initially in favor of the surface. Traveling to examine a sample of the flooring, he informed school administrators that he preferred hard wood, but the UT administration had already agreed to a package deal with a company to install synthetic surfaces on the football field, track and basketball court.

The ostentatious surface proved to be an integral part of the pageantry of Mears' "Greatest Show on Earth."

Would You Buy Insurance Off This Guy?

 During his playing career with the Vols, Ernie Grunfield, an expert at the free throw line, shot several charity tosses for teammates that were fouled. Officials appeared to be oblivious to Ernie G's tactics. In at least one game the ploy could have made the difference.

In the late stages during a Kentucky game, a Vol player was fouled during his shot; Ernie, serving in a surrogate role, stealthily moved to the free throw line. It was evident to almost everyone present except the official who made the call that Grunfeld had not been fouled. Joe Hall, the Kentucky coach, objected vehemently. He attempted to halt play so the officials could make a correction, but his pleas fell on deaf ears as Ernie G. sank both free throws. Later Coach Hall claimed the call made the difference in the game.

Recently when asked whether Ernie was the correct person on the line, Coach Mears remarked: "He had a tendency to take advantage of people any time he had a chance; Ernie had a real knack for this. He was always looking for an opportunity and then he would go for it. That's one of the reasons he was such a great player. I don't really know." Smilingly, Coach continued: "I'd probably let Ernie shoot free throws for me, but I don't know if I'd buy any insurance off him."

Good-Bye, Number One

 In the opening game of the 1969-70 season the Tennessee basketball Vols journeyed to Columbia, South Carolina, to play Frank McGuire's Gamecocks. South Carolina had been tabbed by *Sports Illustrated Magazine* as the pre-season pick for the number one position in the nation.

Tennessee was out-manned in the game as the Gamecocks had a huge front line and some excellent guards to go with them. Frank McGuire had roots in the eastern part of the United States, and many of his players hailed from the New York area. One player on this South Carolina squad, Bobby Cremmins, went on to an outstanding coaching career at Georgia Tech.

Coach Mears recalled the game in this way: "South Carolina had great talent. They were bigger and stronger than us and of course they had that number one ranking and home court advantage. No one gave us much of a chance. In fact, our team was a little down in talent that year. We had Bobby Croft inside, Jimmy England at the point, and Don Johnson on a wing, but they didn't match up well against South Carolina."

The Vols competed with a lot of heart and determination that night in Columbia and came away with a stunning upset. They used a sticky zone defense and a very deliberate offense that forced the Gamecocks to retard their up-tempo playing style. For Coach Mears and his Vols it was an impressive victory, certainly one of the most memorable in the coach's fourteen years at the helm of the Volunteer program. But more importantly, the outcome proved that the Tennessee basketball program was ranked among the most prestigious in the country.

The day of the game Ken Rice, Coach Mears and several Orange Tie Club members were walking the streets of Columbia when Ken noticed a stuffed gamecock for sale in one of the store windows. He told Coach Mears if the Vols won that night he would buy the feathered fowl for him. As the store had closed by the time the game ended, Ken surreptitiously made the purchase. The prized Gamecock with its colorful feathers and razor-sharp claws still perches prominently in the proud Coach's home as a reminder of the night the nation said "good-bye" to a number-one team.

"Beef" Signs the "Show"

Fans have wondered how Coach Mears landed two of the most coveted basketball players from the New York area to Tennessee. Most eastern players stayed at home, attending Syracuse, Niagara or St. Johns University; others gravitated toward coaches that had strong ties in the New York area, such as Frank McGuire at South Carolina, Al McGuire at Marquette, and "Digger" Phelps at Notre Dame. But here is how the "Ernie and Bernie Show" was brought to Big Orange Country.

Respecting Coach Aberdeen, Tommy Konchalski, who scouted high school talent in the East and whose brother played for Coach Aberdeen at Arcadia College in Canada, contacted Stu regarding the highly touted recruits. The Vols had "made their mark" in the East by participating in the NIT, and Coach Aberdeen had eastern connections; both were compelling factors when recruiting New York players. After Konchalski embarked Coach Aberdeen on the King/Grunfeld trail, Stu never wavered. Kentucky and Syracuse recruited Grunfeld intensely; however, the high school All-American became enchanted with the East Tennessee lifestyle and signed with the Vols.

Subsequent to signing Grunfeld, Coach Aberdeen recruited Bernard King with tremendous vigor to the UT campus. Some of the credit for alluring him to come to Tennessee should go to Ernie Grunfeld. Bernard knew little about UT, but he was acquainted with Ernie and quizzed him regarding the Tennessee program. According to Coach Mears, when Bernard asked Ernie what he thought of the Vols, the All-American replied: "They've done everything for me they said they would do and more. It's a great place to play basketball and if you come to Tennessee, you'll never regret it."

Coach Aberdeen signed King, and the Ernie and Bernie show began production.

Oh, What Might Have Been

 Coach Mears recruited some of the most outstanding high school talent in America. The following is a list of a few that "got away":

Kent Benson to Indiana
Mike Flynn to Kentucky
Kevin Grevey to Kentucky
Spencer Hayward to Detroit
Kevin Joyce to South Carolina
Kyle Macey to Purdue/Kentucky
Jerry Memmering to Indiana
Johnny Neumann to Mississippi
Bruce Parkinson to Purdue
Tommy Roy to Maryland

Coach Mears Versus "The General"

Coach Mears' Tennessee Vols played Bobby Knight only twice during Mears' fourteen-year tenure. The first meeting occurred at the 1969 NIT while Knight coached at West Point. That year "The General" had an outstanding guard that was directed to shoot from the corners; however, the Vols' 1-3-1-trap zone defense was strongest in the corners. Therefore, this defensive scheme confused Bob's team, and the Tennessee Volunteers won the game. "It was a great win for us, placing us in third place in the national tournament," Coach Mears remarked.

In 1974 the Vols met Coach Knight (then at Indiana University) again in the post-season National Commissioners Invitational Tournament. The Hoosiers, loaded with talent, featured All-American Kent Benson. Coach Mears' Vols played Coach Knight's Hoosiers head to head once again, but Indiana won the game. The next year "The General's" boys won the NCAA Championship with virtually the same squad.

Peaking with Sports Illustrated

Coach Mears' teams were highly successful at Tennessee but his program only graced the cover of *Sports Illustrated Magazine* one time. Being placed on the cover of this illustrious magazine was the dream of every athlete.

Tennessee's "shining moment" arrived during the Bernard King and Ernie Grunfeld years. The cover depicted the two Tennessee "greats" leaning against the goal post clad in their colorful orange and white warm-up uniforms. Basketball spirits were high on "the hill" and the "Ernie and Bernie Show" provided 12,700 Tennessee fans many hours of competitive entertainment and memorable moments.

Ernie and Bernard, chosen as the two top players in the Southeastern Conference by the Associated Press in 1977, boasted scoring averages that were the envy of their competitors. The *Sports Illustrated* article contributed to their All-American status and established the Vol program among the nation's best. For Coach Mears, his Volunteers had attained their peak.

Who Was the Greatest?

When Coach Mears talks about the premier players that were a part of his basketball program he uses the analogy of branches on a tree. For instance, he would state: "Jim England and Bill Justus were the greatest one-on-one players I had. Mike Edwards and Danny Schultz were my two greatest long-range shooters. Billy Hann and Rodney Woods were my greatest ball handlers. Ron Widby and Ernie Grunfeld were my greatest competitors. Tommy Boerwinkle and Len Kosmalski were my greatest 7' inside players and Larry Robinson and Howard Bayne were my greatest rebounders."

Coach had a way of describing his outstanding players according to his star system, meaning shooters would shoot, rebounders would rebound, ball handlers would handle the ball and passers would pass. When describing Bernard King, there was no comparable analogy. Bernard was not a branch; he was a tree.

According to Coach, "Bernard was the greatest basketball player to ever play at Tennessee and that includes past, present and future. He could do it all: he could pass, rebound, shoot, and handle the ball; plus, he was a fierce competitor. He was the hardest worker I ever saw and the most complete basketball player I ever coached."

A Boy Named Sue

The opening of the 1969-70 SEC season had not gone as the Volunteers had planned as they lost four of their first five games. Although the start had been very disappointing, the team had beaten the pre-season number-one ranked South Carolina Gamecocks in their opening game. Expectations had been high and by losing four SEC games to start the year their chances of winning a conference championship had become an impossibility.

After the fourth conference loss, Coach Aberdeen, believing he could resolve the squad's problem, reasoned that the players were not "tough" enough, not giving a "gut" effort when the game was on the line. So before a practice session he attempted to get the players' attention in hopes they would exercise a more competitive demeanor on the court.

While the players were in their routinely thirty-minute meeting before practice, Coach instructed the managers to align the players' chairs along the sideline with girls' names attached to them. There was a chair for Sue, Jane, Karen, Carol and a host of others.

On arrival at the practice floor, the team's reaction was noticeably unpleasant as some players ripped the names off the chairs, others turned the chairs over and a few chairs were kicked quite a distance. Coach Aberdeen had ignited a fire under his players and immediate results were obvious. The "Boy Named Sue" displayed more competitiveness for the remainder of the season and won some key Southeastern Conference games.

There's Going to Be a Barn Burning

My Dad was an avid basketball fan and possessed a keen wit of basketball knowledge. A typical Hoosier, he became assertive and opinionated while watching a game. Most of the time Dad was correct in his assessments; however, sometimes his vociferous protests appeared at an inopportune time and place.

Subsequent to one of my games as a Volunteer I was headed back to the court for a customary post-game reunion with friends and family when my future wife Debbie came running up toward me obviously perplexed. I asked her, "What's the matter?" Disbelievingly she responded, "You've got to get your Dad out of here; he's telling everyone he's gonna' burn the field house down." Apparently, Dad was not pleased with the way the game had progressed and was venting his frustration, advocating that I should have gotten a few more chances at shooting the ball. Nevertheless, we did get him out of the arena pretty quickly and prevented a barn burning.

You Are On Your Own

On a cold, wintry Friday night several UT basketball players headed to the Tennessee Theatre in downtown Knoxville. A fringe benefit of being a member of the basketball squad included free passes to the local theatres. On this particular night I drove my car and parked the vehicle in one of the lots behind the Tennessee Theatre. After the movie we returned to the car and it refused to start. That car was always trying my patience and on that night it had pushed me to the limit. At times it used so much oil that I used to tell people I would stop at a service station and check the gas and fill it with oil. There was nothing that could be done to the car that night, so we hiked from downtown back to Gibbs Hall.

When I reached the room I called my Dad in Indiana to see if he had a solution to the problem with the vehicle. It was late in the evening when I called and the phone rang seemingly forever. Finally, Dad answered and I said, "Dad, my car's in downtown Knoxville and it won't start." Subsequent to a long silence on the line, he uttered those words I will remember the rest of my life: "Hell, what do you want me to do about it; get in my car and come down there and fix it tonight?" It was at this moment that I came to realize my decision to attend the University of Tennessee had placed me on my own.

I can never remember asking my parents for any favors since.

A State Championship Question

I could not write a book about basketball stories without including a few tales from the Indiana Hoosier hardwood. The next several stories are a few of my favorites.

In the early sixties a high school in Indiana had an outstanding player who was rated one of the best in the state. His school was one of the premier squads in Hoosier Land at that time and had advanced to the finals at Indianapolis. The dream of every team was to play before 14,000 fans in Butler Field House known as the "Big Barn."

The whole town was excited with their tournament advancement, but they had a problem: The star player had failed geography and would be ineligible to participate in the State Tournament. The coach, knowing their chances of winning were nil without the outstanding participant, went to the school's administrators to discuss the possibility of giving the All Stater some make-up work. Everyone was in agreement with the additional work except the geography teacher who, in her academic excellence, tried to explain that the ineligible player had his chance but did not apply himself.

After much discussion ensued, a compromise was reached. The troubled roundballer would be given one question; if he got it correct, he would be allowed to participate in the state tournament. The anxious player was administered the question. The room was full of witnesses—the teacher, coach, athletic director, principal, a few school board members and a couple of fans. This test question was probably the most decisive one ever asked at the basketball-loving school. The teacher looked at the student and inquired, "Son, what is the capital of Indiana?" After several minutes of deep thought and pondering the weight of the question, he hesitantly answered: "Anderson." Everyone in the room was stunned. The teacher replied, "Son, I'm sorry; the answer is Indianapolis." "Hell fire," screamed the Coach, "Give me a map." After studying the map closely and approximating that Anderson was thirty-five to forty miles from Indianapolis, he looked at the teacher and suggested, "What if we take one point off for each mile Anderson is from Indianapolis?"

The teacher replied, "Well, Coach, he missed it by thirty-five to forty miles; that would give him a score of 60 or 65 and still would not place him above the 70 grade mark which is required for passing." The Coach began to smile and pleadingly said, "Well, let's curve it."

The "eligible" player starred in the State Tournament and the Hoosier community won it all.

No Offense

We had just lost the New Castle Sectional finals in Indiana with over 12,000 fans witnessing the game in the largest high school gym in the world. It was my junior season in high school; and we had just completed another outstanding year without a sectional championship, much to the disappointment of our players and fans. The finale had been close for a couple of quarters; but the tide turned when New Castle went on a shooting spree and we ended up losing the game by around twenty points.

After the contest the players and coaches gathered on the floor to await the team bus. Our head coach, Joe Stanley, was as disappointed as all of us and probably a little more so since Indiana basketball can be stressful on coaches even when they are winning. Standing directly behind Joe was one of our fans, an elderly lady probably in her seventies. She was not a "happy trooper," as the game had left a bitter taste in her mouth. Just when the team manager yelled, "Bus is here," Coach Stanley abruptly turned around and bumped directly into the frail basketball devotee, almost knocking her to the floor. Startled, Coach Stanley raised both of his arms, looked at the poor lady, and apologized; "I'm sorry, Ma'am; no offense!" The elderly Greenfield fan retorted with a sarcastic reply: "That's right and not a helluva lot of defense either, Coach Stanley."

Hot Game, Cold Ride Home

Two Indiana basketball referees pulled their cars into a school parking lot, attempting to find a convenient spot. Parking sites on this night were scarce due to the opposing team's bus that was parked in the lot along with the cars of other personnel. The visibility in the lot was diminished as the result of a four-inch snowfall with flakes continuing to pepper down.

As they approached the rear of the gym, the referees became pleasantly surprised as they saw two signs distinctly marked: "Game Referees Only" along with two spaces where the snow had been neatly shoveled to the side. As they pulled into the spaces and got out, one of the referees remarked, "This is real Hoosier hospitality." The other referee agreed: "It's been a long time since I've been given this kind of respect on a basketball night."

The game was hotly contested with the home team and visiting team exchanging leads several times over the course of the game. In the thirty-two minutes of play there were several questionable calls and the two "refs" were feeling the heat. In the closing seconds a call was whistled against the home team, giving the visiting squad possession of the ball that resulted in their scoring the winning basket at the final buzzer. The two "refs" sprinted off the court as fans' conduct in the gym became unruly.

Feeling the urgency for a quick escape, the referees skipped their customary showers but were delayed from leaving the premises by the school's principal and athletic director who wanted to query them regarding the outcome of the game. After ten minutes or so the "refs," who were eager to leave due to the worsening weather conditions, explained to the administrators that they had a long drive and needed to go. As they exited the back gym door and approached their cars, they could not believe their eyes: Both of their cars had been vandalized with snow being packed from top to bottom in the interior.

Officiating Indiana high school basketball could be harsh on referees, especially to ones who had privileged parking spaces when the home team lost.

Thumbs Up for the "Refs"

My high school coach at Greenfield, Indiana, Mel Garland—a marvelous basketball player at Indianapolis Tech High School—became an All-Big-Ten performer at Purdue. He was later enshrined in the Indiana Basketball Hall of Fame. Unfortunately, he passed away in his early forties from cancer. Coach Garland was a tremendous influence on my basketball career and not many days pass that I do not think about him.

During Mel's college playing days at Purdue, as team captain he was responsible for providing leadership as well as being a proper role model to the younger kids. But the task he had to perform before one of the Boilermaker home games was beyond the call of duty.

A problem with crowd behavior had developed at the school that included harsh and unsportsmanlike conduct toward the referees. Purdue had tried several methods to alleviate the problem—articles in the newspaper, short spots on TV with pleas from the athletic director, and discontinuing the introduction of officials prior to the games. None of the strategies worked; in fact, the crowd behavior seemed to worsen with each contest as the sportsmanlike tactics were tried.

Garland, a clean-cut Indiana boy with an All-American appearance, was popular among the Boilermaker faithful. Extremely loyal to Purdue, very personable and well liked by his teammates, he was the epitome of the perfect captain.

Before one of the games, Ray Eddy, the head coach of the Boilermakers, suggested to Mel, "I would like for you to go to the court, take the microphone and talk to the student body about the importance of sportsmanship." The soft spoken and shy lad felt, as captain of the team, obligated to fulfill the request.

Taking the microphone, Mel, pleading with the students, said, "The referees have one of the most important jobs on the court; the game could not be played without them and they are men of integrity, always trying to do their best just as the players. They deserve your respect." Even Mel believed the speech was effective; however, the crowd made no immediate response.

Garland returned to the locker room and Coach Eddy asked, "How did everything go?" Mel replied, "Great; I don't think there will be any further problems."

When the Boilermaker squad took to the court to warm up, the Purdue student body booed them for five minutes; however, when the referees entered the arena, the crowd greeted them with a resounding ten-minute standing ovation. It was Mel's last speech on sportsmanship.

Nailed

Mel Garland, my former high school coach, taught mechanical drawing at Greenfield High School. The teacher's desk in the classroom was wooden. One day at the conclusion of lunch period and just before Mel's class was to begin, Chuck Rodee, one of his students, took Mel's teaching textbook and nailed it securely to the instructor's desk, carefully turning the pages so the nails were not visible.

Mel, unaware of the prank, was not able to pry the book from the desk or turn the pages. His frustration extended into basketball practice later that day as he "nailed" us with a rigorous workout.

Touching Lives

 While serving as a teacher/coach at Farragut High School in Knoxville, Tennessee, I had a student who had failed my class three consecutive terms. On enrollment day showing intense persistence, this student came into my class for a fourth try.

I questioned the student by saying, "Mario, have you got me again?" He replied, "Yes, Coach, I surely do." Distrusting his motives, I then quizzed him, "Are you going to put forth a better effort this time?" To which he replied, "I'm going to try." He did not sound convincing, so I said, "Mario, you have been in my class three straight terms and you have failed all three. We have other teachers in this department you could choose." He replied, "I know, Coach, but I asked to be put in your class." "You failed me three times and still want to take me?" I asked. He then answered, "I sure do; are you going to show that movie *Hoosiers* again?"

I guess Indiana basketball touches a lot of lives in many different ways.

Overrated

During the annual Indiana/Kentucky summer classic, George McGinnis, Indiana's Mr. Basketball, had scored twenty-three points in the first match-up at Indianapolis. The Hoosier team had defeated the Blue Grass Boys by a score of 91-83 before 14,700 fans. Many sportswriters, due to his low shooting percentage, considered big George's performance sub-par for him. Joe Voskuhl went a step farther, telling a Louisville sports reporter that George was overrated and that Indiana was not good enough to beat Kentucky a second time. The broad-shouldered, 225-pound charger from Covington Catholic High School made a bold prediction. He said, "McGinnis will not get twenty-three points off of me this time around in Louisville."

Before 18,000 fans in Louisville Freedom Hall, Joe Voskuhl's prediction of George not getting twenty-three points became a reality. McGinnis performed magnificently as he scored fifty-three points and grabbed thirty rebounds to lead Indiana to a 114-83 win over Kentucky. What was most remarkable was the fact he blew out one side of one of his basketball shoes in the process and the managers could not provide a replacement. He played the entire second half with half a shoe. As a participant on the high school and college level, I had never witnessed a greater individual and team offensive exhibition.

As for Joe Voskuhl, the best advice one could have offered him at the time was: If you can't think of anything positive to say about somebody, it might be wise not to say anything, especially if the guy you are talking about was one of the most spectacular players to have ever graced the hardwood in Indiana.

A Man with a Plan

 No Volunteer in history shot free throws more accurately than Tennessee All-American Bill Justus. In 1968-69 Bill led the nation in free-throw percentage, hitting 92 per cent of his attempts. The deadly outside shooting wingman had a special routine when he went to the charity stripe.

He initially stood back from the line; then he pulled up both socks, one at a time. The tug up of his socks was a part of the routine that served the purpose of drying his hands. When handed the ball by the official, he raised the ball back over his head with both hands, while loosening his shoulders. He then bounced the ball with both hands—three times before the first shot; two times before the second. Bill always placed the shooting "fork" (i.e., the index and middle fingers) under the ball logo (Spaulding 100) so that the laces would be in perfect rotation on the shot. Taking a deep inhale and exhale, he aimed for the front of the rim and let it fly.

Then John Ward, the "Voice of the Vols," gave his stamp of approval, "Bottom!"

Rise and Fall in the Classroom

 I had completed four consecutive quarters of English on the Knoxville campus and was fortunate to have earned grades of either A or B. I found English grammar and literature classes to be quite fascinating and I enjoyed writing.

That was to change during the winter quarter of my sophomore year. On my first two written themes in an English class I received grades of an F and a D. I informed my instructor that I would not be attending class on Monday due to a basketball trip; remaining consistent with her, I received two more failing grades. I reasoned that the instructor might have had some unpleasant experiences with athletes in the past and was holding a grudge.

Nevertheless, I was confused because I did not think my efforts had diminished from the prior term; so I took the essays to a previous English instructor for her to peruse. After analyzing my themes, she informed me the papers deserved a letter grade no lower than B. She then presented my written work to the head of the English department but no action was taken. Their recommendation was that I drop the course and pick it up next quarter, which I did.

Even though I had knowledgeable instructors at the University of Tennessee and obtained a first-class education, there were times, such as these, that I somewhat regretted I had pursued a basketball career.

The Value of a Dollar

Subsequent to winning a key Southeastern Conference game at home, my future wife Debbie and I were dining with friends to celebrate the victory. As we were leaving the restaurant a man called my name and motioned for me to come to his table. He and his wife had been dining with another couple and they all appeared to be "high rollers." Stating that they had attended the game, he congratulated me on the win and my performance. I thanked him for his complimentary remarks.

As I turned to leave, he stuck out his hand to shake mine; and as our hands met, he placed money in my grasp and said, "Mike, take your girlfriend out to supper on me." He made this offer so all in his party could hear. Although flattered, I informed him that it was against the NCAA rules to accept gifts. Returning the money to him, I noticed that he had presented me with a one-dollar bill.

The people in his group began laughing in regard to the incident that embarrassed me. When I got back to Debbie and our friends, she asked, "What was that all about?" I replied, "I just scored 25 points to help us win a key Southeastern Conference game, and that jerk over there thought it was worth a buck."

Yikes! I'm in a Foreign Land

 It never failed—every time I had a math class on "the hill," I was placed with an instructor of foreign descent. Now do not get me wrong, I have nothing against foreigners, but math was difficult enough for me without adding to my frustration by having a teacher with a foreign accent.

In one particular math class I did not remain very long. On the first day of class the foreign instructor, going down the rows collecting personal information from his students, came to me, and asked, "What is your name?" I replied, "Edwards." He then queried, "Edwards—how do you spell that?"

Well, you do not get any more English than "Edwards," and if he could not spell that, it was time for me to head for the "Drop and Add Line."

Merry Christmas

Our Tennessee Basketball Team was scheduled to fly out of Knoxville on December 25, 1971, to play in a holiday tournament in New York City, making it impossible for me to spend Christmas with my family in Indiana. Traditionally, Christmas was a special occasion at the Edwards' house so naturally I was a little homesick.

Preceding the trip, my future in-laws invited me to celebrate the holidays with them. Subsequent to a delicious Christmas Eve dinner, Debbie (my future wife) and I attempted to convince her parents to delay their custom of opening gifts until Christmas morning, but her Dad was determined to unwrap them on Christmas Eve.

During the discussion, the telephone rang. Deb's Mom answered the phone but hung up the receiver immediately, not saying a word. Deb's Dad asked her, "Who was that?" She replied, "Someone who is sick." "What did they say?" he questioned. She answered, "They said, 'Merry Christmas; you'll all be dead in the morning.'"

Even though the call did not appear to affect Deb's Dad, I was upset and ready to leave for New York immediately—forget Christmas. He nonchalantly looked at us and insisted, "If we're all going to be dead in the morning, we better get these gifts opened tonight."

That was one Christmas Eve I did not get much sleep—not because of the excitement of Santa Claus's arrival or the ensuing trip to New York.

Going Fishing

The Georgia Bulldogs were not playing to their potential; therefore, their Coach Ken Rosemond attempted a new approach in motivating his team. He had tried several impelling techniques during the season, but the Bulldogs just would not respond. The team appeared to be on vacation, losing one SEC game after another.

Rosemond, frustrated with his squad, boarded the plane to Mississippi for a game while toting his fishing gear. The players took one look at him and asked, "Coach, what are you doing?" Rosemond replied, "This team's been on vacation all year, so I thought I would take one." Coach Rosemond believed the tactic would inspire his squad to play harder, but, instead, they "laid down on the job" and lost again.

At the conclusion of the season Coach Rosemond had plenty of time to fish as Georgia terminated his contract.

Welcome to the Big Leagues, Boy

 During Coach Mears' tenure with the Volunteers, the Orange and White pre-season intra-squad game, played prior to Thanksgiving, gave fans their first look at the squad. To provide excitement and competition, teams were divided equally. Coach Mears had the varsity exhibit their Globetrotter warm-up drills, and the band and cheerleaders performed, simulating an actual game atmosphere. This contest would be the final performance in front of a crowd before the season opener.

Mears allowed the Freshmen Team to participate in order to gain game experience. As a freshman, excited to wear the orange and white uniform for the first time, I was placed on Captain Jimmy England's White Team and was slated to guard veteran player Don Johnson.

Johnson showed me the difference between high school and college basketball competition in a hurry. He made shots from the right side of the court, the left side of the court, the right corner, the left corner, and the top of the key; he even hit all his free throws when I fouled him. The harder I worked on defense, the more points he scored. The performance was Don's way of welcoming me to the "big leagues."

Coach, We're Not in Rome

Coach Mears won his 300th game during the 1972 season. The win came in Starkville, Mississippi, against the Bulldogs. As the final buzzer sounded, the Volunteer Team carried their Coach from the floor in celebration of his coaching milestone. However, the Mississippi crowd was not in a festive mood due to their loss, and seeing a team carry a coach, whom they were not fond of, off their floor stirred up anger.

As the team headed to the locker room with Coach Mears on their shoulders, the Bulldog fans began pelting them with whatever they could find in the stands. Paper cups were hurled, programs rocketed, and popcorn boxes and paper wrappings were all seen flying by Coach's head.

In Roman times pomp and ceremony accompanied the triumphant gladiators as they were carried out of the arena with trumpets sounding and flowers being thrown. However, Mississippi State was not part of the Roman Empire.

What to Do with a Three-Hundred-Win Coach

Subsequent to his 300th win at Mississippi State, Coach Mears was placed on the team's shoulders as they carried him to the locker room. On arriving at the destination, the players faced a dilemma: Do we place him on the bench in the locker room? Do we put him in a chair? Do we set him on his feet? Do we throw him up in the air and yell? None of us had been through this type of celebration before, but quick-thinking Steve Hirschorn provided the solution, "Let's throw him in the shower."

Some of us were not sure this action would be exercising wisdom since we had to practice the next day. But before we could arrive at a consensus, Steve had Coach headed for the shower stalls. Hirsch, leading the charge, chose the cold spigot instead of turning on the warm faucet.

The players, with outstretched arms not wanting any part of the cold water, held Coach until he was completely soaked, and shivering had set in. After the cold shower, his players abandoned the drenching wet "celebrity."

Coach Mears seemed to enjoy the celebration, so the action of the team commemorating their coach's 300th victory must have been appropriate.

Guys Named Eddie

During my high school years I had a teammate by the name of Eddie Bodkin who guarded me during practice. He would hold me, elbow me, trip me, push me, grab my jersey, call me names, and do whatever it required to make me a better player. Eddie, taking satisfaction in upsetting me, enjoyed his ability to fluster my composure. One of the milestones in my life was when my basketball career at Greenfield High School in Indiana ended and I no longer had to face Eddie Bodkin in those practice sessions.

However, my excitement of losing Eddie was short lived because when I became a Tennessee Volunteer another Eddie—Eddie Voelker, guarded me in practice. This Eddie proved to be more aggressive than the first. Voelker, a fierce competitor with anxious anticipation, would enter the practice floor to exhibit his defensive skills at my expense. Holding, shoving, pushing, and elbowing were all in a day's work for Eddie.

Both Eddies contributed to the improvement of my basketball skills. But after eight years of being physically and mentally challenged by guys named Eddie, I swore that if I ever had a son he would not be named Eddie.

Pops

During the early 1970's a favorite watering hole for UT students and especially UT athletes was the Varsity Inn on the Cumberland Strip. The walls of this pub, owned by the Kampas Family—Pops, Gus and Victor—were adorned with pictures of UT athletes and reflected the owners' support for the Vols.

For several years, Gus and Victor reserved basketball season tickets for front row seats behind the goal at Stokely, and they usually spent game nights harassing the officials. In fact, they seemed to be so familiar with the officials that they called them by their first names. Well, let's put it this way, they called them by their first names at the start of the game; but by game's end if things were not going well for the Vols, the Kampas boys would call them unflattering names.

The Kampas Family was of Greek origin. Victor and Gus spoke English fluently but Pops was not as familiar with the English language as his sons. However, he did know how to count money.

A customer was unable to exit the Varsity Inn without passing Pops at the cash register. Nevertheless, students who were cognizant of his language handicap and attempted to take advantage of him regarding their food bill discovered it was a losing proposition. Pops counted every penny; and when it came to money, he was a whiz of the English language.

266

"Thanks a Lot"

 Coach Mears' Volunteers had just beaten Adolph Rupp and his Kentucky "Runts" to hand them their first and only loss of the entire season. Upon arriving at his office the following day, the exuberant Coach Mears was informed that the UT Athletic Director wanted to see him.

Coach rushed to the AD's office, presuming that he was going to receive a salary increase or at the least a congratulatory "pat on the back" regarding the outstanding victory of the previous night. Instead, the Athletic Director informed him that he was cutting his basketball-recruiting budget several thousand dollars as the money was needed for other sports' programs.

Coach's team had just beaten the number one team in the country and his reward was a reduction of his program funds. Coach Mears made a call to UT President Andy Holt informing him of the situation. One call later the attempted basketball budget cut was history.

Should'a Come West

In 1971 the Vols had participated in the Trojan Classic in Los Angeles, California, and were passing through the airport terminal to catch a flight. As I wound my way through the busy corridor, an outstretched hand grabbed my right arm. It was Denny Crum, the assistant coach of the UCLA Bruins. He looked at me and said, "You should have come out here to play with us; you would be playing now. Our guards aren't performing worth a crap." The Bruins were returning from a holiday tournament in Pittsburgh and obviously the coaching staff was not pleased with the performance of their guards.

It was just a couple of years before that Coach John Wooden and Assistant Coach Denny Crum had visited my home in Greenfield, Indiana, in hopes that I would decide to attend their school. Coach Wooden, a native of Martinsville, Indiana, preferred to have at least one Hoosier on his squad. I visited UCLA as a high school senior but decided it was in my best interest to sign with the Vols.

Coach Crum that day in the airport informed me that Coach Wooden and he, upon following my career, were pleased I was doing well. In the mid-1990's I wrote Coach Wooden a letter bringing him up to date on my post-college career. I also asked if he recalled visiting Greenfield, Indiana, in1969. In a few days I received a two-page, handwritten letter from him thanking me for my note. He related that he remembered it well, having only visited five recruits in their home during his entire coaching career and one of those homes was in Greenfield, Indiana.

A Man's Best Friend

 Stu Aberdeen, the fiery assistant coach of the Tennessee Volunteers in charge of defensive schemes, owned three dogs of which he was very fond. There was Red Dog, Big Dog and Mad Dog.

When playing opposing teams and attempting to disrupt their play, Coach would fetch Red Dog (full-court-man-to-man defense). If he wanted a more physically defensive performance, he would whistle for Big Dog (full-court-zone defense). And if he became highly irritated with the opposing team, he would sic Mad Dog on them, his fiercest and most beloved dog (full-court-run-and-jump defense).

The clever Coach utilized his "best friends" scheme astutely.

A Trip to Victoria's Secret

 During one particular practice session the inside players of the Vols were not performing aggressively enough to suit Coach Stu Aberdeen, the defensive coordinator. Referring to the playing of his inside "horsemen" as "sissy-like," he also labeled their performance as "girl-like" play.

The exasperated Coach stopped practice and, turning to Manager Jerry McClanahan, asked, "Where's the closest lingerie store located to the gym?" The somewhat puzzled manager, looking a little embarrassed, answered, "I guess down on the Cumberland Strip." "Good," Stu replied, "Go down and get me some lacy panties and bras for these guys; make sure they are really lacy." Shyly, McClanahan queried, "What size and colors should I get?" Stu, unaccustomed to purchasing women's lingerie, responded, "The biggest they've got—in pink, and make certain they pack them in a frilly box." McClanahan, still confused, asked, "How do I pay for it?"

Coach Aberdeen who was big on strategies but short on cash, replied, "Hold just a second; let's see if we can get these guys a little more macho in the next drill."

A Ray Mears Tradition— Playing Sick

The Tennessee Volunteers were preparing to compete against the Michigan Wolverines and the flu bug had engulfed one of Ray Mears stalwart players—Wes Coffman. Wes was confined to the motel room with a temperature above 102 degrees. Mears had given the Volunteer the morning and afternoon to recover and told him, "Wes, you can sit out the shooting practice this morning, but I expect you in uniform for the game tonight." Poor Wes could barely get out of bed to regurgitate.

Coffman, in recalling his preparation for the Wolverines and his defensive assignment, stated: "It was all I could do to get my uniform on, let alone thinking about the man Coach wanted me to guard—All American Cazzie Russell. I had no energy at all." Right before the tip off Coach Mears said to Wes, "Now I know you're not feeling well, but you'll forget about being sick after the game starts, and we'll give you some rest."

"Coach Mears never gave me any reprieve during the contest. I played the entire forty minutes trying to manhandle Cazzie Russell. However, I did take great pride in holding the Wolverine under his offensive average. He had been scoring at a thirty-two-point clip, and I held him to thirty-one," Wes jokingly remarked.

The Drinks Are on Me

In 1992, the Tennessee Volunteer Basketball Team held a twenty-five year reunion commemorating their SEC Championship. At the conclusion of the meal and program, the former players headed for a room to view a film of their championship game with Mississippi State. Shortly before the film started, one of the players, Kerry "Killer" Myers, placed an order to the bar to bring several cases of Jack Daniels, beer, and other distilled spirits to the room. When the bartenders delivered the beverages, Kerry stood and shouted, "The drinks are on me!"

A short time later the hotel manager brought the exorbitant bill to the room and asked, "Who gets the check?" All the players pointed to Kerry who then motioned the bill bearer to deliver the invoice to him. "Killer," taking one glance at the astronomical debt, removed his pen from his coat pocket, and without hesitation signed: "Doug Dickey, Athletic Director, University of Tennessee."

Wrap It in a Towel

In 1967 Tennessee was entering an unprecedented third overtime period against Mississippi State in Starkville. The team was in a quest for a SEC Championship, and John Ward, the Voice of the Vols, had a major problem—his voice was dissipating. The flamboyant play-by-play radio announcer had blurted too many "give it to him's!" "bottoms!" and "bangs!" A cold breeze through an open window in the field house also contributed to his hoarseness.

A voice that had been trained to go forty minutes had abruptly lost its energy. Knowing that the completion of the thrilling contest needed to be relayed to the hills of East Tennessee, Ward asked Lowell Blanchard of WNOX to take the microphone and describe the final action during a time out. Blanchard declined and in an attempt to calm the frustrated Ward, he frantically grabbed a loose towel on the scorer's table and wrapped it around the panicky sportscaster's throat in an attempt to keep his vocals warm. The technique worked and Ward finished the play by play of the most exciting Vol basketball game of the Ray Mears era.

From that night until the end of his broadcasting career, John Ward always wore a towel draped firmly around his neck while describing the action of Vol football and basketball games. By grabbing a towel that had been discarded next to him, Lowell Blanchard had initiated a Tennessee tradition and a John Ward trademark.

That's Not a Pass

Mike Edwards had just attempted a thirty-foot jump shot as the SEC official signaled a foul on the defender. Not being familiar with Edwards' long-range attempts, the referee approached the scorer's table and stated, "That's a foul on the defender on the pass." Russ Bebb, the official scorer seated at the table, looked astonishingly at the official and replied, "That's impossible—Edwards has never thrown a pass in his entire career at UT."

Looks Aren't Everything

 During the 1969-70 Volunteer basketball season, All-American point guard Jimmy England sustained an injury to his thigh. The bruise was so deep that England had to play with a great deal of pain. The ice and heat treatment, given by trainer Mickey O'Brien, proved to be ineffective.

To keep the Vol standout from reinjurying the leg in practice or a game Mick put to use his football training expertise. He designed a device to pad the bruise. The Vol trainer took a thigh pad from a pair of football pants and taped the cushion to England's upper leg. The crude device proved effective as England played the remainder of the year without further injury. Mick's thigh apparatus was the ugliest health device ever placed on a Vol basketballer. That is probably the major reason ole Mick never marketed it.

Silence for Roger

When Coach Mears selected Roger Peltz to ride the unicycle in the Vols' pre-game warm-ups, the Vol mentor should have taken out an insurance policy on the 6'5" player. While learning to manipulate the one-wheeled contraption, the determined Peltz took some nasty falls in the hallway of Stokely Athletic Center. While other Vol players were performing shooting drills, Rog would practice getting on the unicycle, which was no easy task. He would hug the corridor walls with his arms as he attempted to glide the vehicle forward.

As players shot their balls in the gym, they could hear the frustrated Peltz getting off and on the unicycle in an attempt to master his riding skills. At times the uncooperative vehicle would go one way and Peltz would be bounced in another. He took some horrifying spills. The loudest noise and the most concern, however, occurred when Peltz would lose his balance and run the cycle directly into a loosely stationed garbage can. Upon this collision all balls in the gym were quieted and the players stood motionless as if to be offering Roger a befitting moment of silence.

It's Fiesta Time

The 1962 Tennessee Vol Basketball Team was preparing to play in the Sun Bowl Tournament in El Paso, Texas. It was Ray Mears' first year at the helm. A group of Volunteer players led by Pat Robinette and Orb E. Bowling decided to rent a station wagon and head across the border into Juarez, Mexico. Orb was the "class clown" of the trip as he made jokes about the barren countryside and a culture that was very un-Tennessean. Ole Orb, a gangling figure, stood a good 6'10", and Robinette and the other players used to joke with the Ichabod Crane-looking-figure by claiming his nose protruded to at least 6'9".

Nevertheless, on this excursion Orb was having the time of his life. He and the other members of the Vol team attended a bull fight, visited local markets, and saw cactus plants galore. Even Orb got in the mood by purchasing a large sombrero that only enhanced his comical appearance.

Before entering Mexico, the border guard emphasized to the group that when they returned, they must tell the border gatekeeper that they are Americans. As the Volunteer group approached the gate to exit Mexico, the guard asked the question: "What country?" To which Orb jokingly replied: "I am from national Russia." The 5'8" border guard became hysterical, blowing his whistle and motioning for more security assistance. The gatekeeper began to question Orb and ordered him out of the car. The previously whimsical Orb now became quite concerned. He did not speak Spanish, so communication was impossible. Pat Robinette and the other players did a great job of "comforting" Orb by telling him that he was going to spend the rest of his life in a Mexican prison. Orb survived the ordeal and lived to play another day for the Volunteers as a free man.

Oops! Wrong Number

The Tennessee Vols were in Gainesville, Florida, to play the Gators in a key SEC game. The Sunday before the Monday night contest, the Vols were lounging around the motel with the rest of the Tennessee entourage. Harry Bettis, the owner of Bettis Oil Company in Knoxville, had made the trip with his attractive wife.

A group of Tennessee players were gazing out the motel lobby windows, looking in the direction of the swimming pool where a "knockout" gal was sunning by the pool. Suddenly, Harry Bettis walked by and said, "What's going on here?" One of the Vols said, "We're looking at the blonde by the pool; ain't she something?" Harry looked at the player and asked, "Would you like to meet her?" His face lit up and he anxiously replied, "I sure would." Harry invited the player to meet him in the motel restaurant at 6:30 p.m. for dinner. "I will arrange everything," said Harry. The excited Volunteer returned to his room, put on his Sunday best clothes and prepared for the evening.

As the player entered the dining area of the restaurant, Harry motioned him over to his table where the gorgeous blonde sat. As the Volunteer basketballer was about to approach and introduce himself, Harry connivingly smiled and said, "I would like to introduce you to my wife."

And Down the Stretch They Come

In an attempt to get through the Atlanta Airport first, Marvin West, sportswriter for the *Knoxville News-Sentinel,* and Haywood Harris, of the UT Sports Information Department, decided to stage a race. The event was held at the unusual time of 2 a.m. Both individuals were a little short on track skills, but their competitiveness seemed to get the better of their common sense.

The race proceeded as both participants moved their arms and legs as fast as they could. A.W. Davis, Coach Mears' stalwart center, was drafted by his teammates to serve as the designated finish line, but neither runner was aware of the location.

Observing A. W. standing alone, Haywood assumed that the site where the tall center was stationed was indeed the winner's stripe. Arriving at the coveted line, he leaned forward for the victory. However, Haywood got too close to Davis, lost his balance, and fell awkwardly to the floor. Marvin West was declared the winner.

Except for Haywood, Coach laughed as hard as anyone. For the Tennessee basketball family, not all the competition was on the court.

It Only Takes a Shot

During Mike Edwards' induction into the Indiana Basketball Hall of Fame, his son Brett was having a discussion with Hoosier hardwood legend, Bobby Plump. Plump became immortal when he hit the game-winning shot against Muncie Central to give tiny Milan the state championship in 1954. The movie *Hoosiers* was based on Bobby's last second heroics.

During the conversation with Edwards' son, Bobby asked, "How many points did your dad score during his high school career?" Brett answered, "I believe he scored 2,343 points." "Damn," Plump replied, "I only hit a shot!"

Make It Short

Former Vol Mike Edwards' son Brett was talking with an Indiana Basketball Hall of Famer, and during the conversation, the former standout asked, "Brett, how does your dad feel about being inducted into the Indiana Basketball Hall of Fame?" Brett replied, "He's really excited but he is a little concerned about his acceptance speech; the Hall asked the recipients to limit their talk to one and a half minutes. But Dad timed his and it was going to consume four minutes."

The elated Hoosier legend responded, "I'll take that; last year some guy talked for one hour, and I downed a whole lot of 'Jack' before he finished."

Did Walt Disney Play for the Vols?

Coach Mears was a stickler for basketball details. He was always trying to outwit the opposing coaches when it came to strategy. Jump ball situations consumed a lot of practice time, and the Vol mentor knew a game could be won or lost with one toss of the ball. In the 60's and early 70's all jump ball situations were honored. There were no alternate possessions.

In Coach Mears' first year he was reviewing jump ball strategies in practice. Verifying the players understood their instructed responsibilities, he asked one of the players, Orb Bowling, "What would you do now?" Orb hesitated in his answer. The lanky center looked around and scratched his chin which irritated Coach Mears who had just spent ten minutes going over the strategy. Adhering to a time schedule was vital to the disciplined coach, and Orb's lack of response was disrupting. Finally, the Vol made his reply, "What would you do, Coach?" A frustrated Mears then ordered the squad back to the meeting room for a more intensive review of jump ball strategies. The practice schedule was shot for the day.

After the session, the team was sent back to the court and assembled once more for the jump ball situation. Coach Mears repeated his question to Orb, "What do you do now?" Orb, looking around the court and randomly selecting a fellow Vol, said, "It depends on what 'Walt' does."

Tennessee had a player by the name of Mike Disney, and all the other squad members nicknamed him "Walt." In his first season Coach Mears had mastered all his players' names; however, he was unfamiliar with their nicknames. Orb never knew Disney's first name; it was always "Walt." With a puzzled expression on his face and a sense of misunderstanding, Coach Mears asked, "What, Orb?" The Vol replied, "It depends on what Walt does." "Who?" retorted the agitated Vol mentor. Ole Orb extending his arm and emphatically pointing to a fellow Vol player answered, "Walt, Walt Disney, standing right there!"

Orb Bowling never knew Mike Disney's first name. He was always known as "Walt" to the lanky Vol center.

The Phantom of the Court

In the early 60's the Vols had a tremendous outside shooter and ballhandler by the name of Danny Schultz. One day in practice the squad was preparing to work against the half court trap defense. Coach Mears wanted everything to be as realistic as possible, so he had Schultz receive the inbound pass from the far end of the court.

The crafty guard retrieved the pass and proceeded to dribble to the left; then he quickly changed directions as to shake the most tenacious defender. With a head fake to the right and a head fake to the left, the Vol All American was in the battle of his life in an attempt to shake an invisible defender and advance the ball to half court.

The realism was taking longer than Coach Mears approved, so he abruptly stopped Schultz and asked, "Danny, what are you doing?" Danny looked at the Vol taskmaster with puzzlement and replied, "Coach, I've got to get past that imaginary man."

A lot of great players have performed against the invisible man in practice, competing against the ghost at boys' clubs, YMCA's, schoolyard courts, high school gyms, and in driveways. The practice phantom and a player placing himself in imaginary game situations have led many basketball dreamers down the road to stardom.

On a cold wintry day in the early 60's, the phantom showed up for a UT basketball practice, and Danny Schultz introduced his friend to Coach Mears. It was probably the first ghost to ever delay a UT basketball practice. Danny did not mind, though, because the phantom helped him to become one of the greatest outside shooters in Vol history and All American status.

"Outside" Shooters

During one of Coach Mears' fall coaching clinics he had a discussion with one of the Tennessee high school coaches who was excited about his upcoming season. He bragged to Coach Mears that he currently possessed the greatest outside shooters ever. Since Coach Mears was always on the lookout to recruit great *outside* shooters for his Star System, he was very impressed with the high school coach's claim.

The conversation came to an abrupt end when the sly high school coach explained, "There is only one problem, though; all our games will be played *inside.*"

Seals Are Loose in the Locker Room

It was December of 1964 and the Vol basketball team was preparing to play Oregon in the Far West Classic. The Orangemen had a squad member by the name of Gil Monroe who later became a warden at Brushy Mountain Prison. He got to know James Earl Ray and others on a personal basis.

Gil was a perfectionist at spinning the basketball on his finger, so he was a natural for Coach Mears' pre-game Globetrotter warm-up show. While in the locker room with no coaches around, Gil decided to put on a show. He started his performance by spinning the ball on his finger and then jumping the ball from hand to hand while continuing to spin. He then reclined on a bench and slowly mounted the ball on his nose. The Vol players went wild, clapping and cheering him on.

Suddenly Coach Mears entered the room, and as if a four star general had made his appearance, the cheering abruptly ceased. Players stood at attention. Gil, on his back, looking at the ceiling with ball spinning on his nose blurted, "Hey guys, where is all the applause?" The usually serious and stern Coach Mears gazed at the clowning Monroe and answered, "Gil, why don't you just go 'Arf, Arf', like a seal?"

A Human Sacrifice

Skip Plotnicki was a nineteen-year-old sophomore and had concluded his freshman season with a stellar performance against Kentucky by scoring twenty points without missing a shot. For Skip it was a career game. His point total equaled the output of future Vol All American A. W. Davis who also tallied twenty points in the game. It had been the second contest in a row that Plotnicki had tied A. W. for game scoring honors.

But the first practice of Plonicki's sophomore year proved to be a reality check when he became a living example of a Coach Mears' point of emphasis. It was the first official practice for the Vol mentor at Tennessee. During a three-man-weave drill that ran the length of the court, Skip received a low pass at the conclusion of the weave and was forced to try a reverse lay-up. The maneuver that Plotnicki attempted was quite creative and possessed an ample amount of "English" (extra spin). The fancy shot slid through the net and the ball did not have time to reach the floor before the colorful Coach was blowing his whistle in disgust. Plotnicki swore he blew it for thirty minutes. Mears gave Skip one of his most notable trademarks, the icy stare—the glance that could melt a player in seconds. The fiery mentor glared at Plotnicki and yelled, "I don't ever want to see a shot like that again!"

Coach was highly intelligent and a great psychiatrist. If his star player, A. W. Davis, had taken that shot, Mears would have said nothing, but when he saw the chance to get a point across to the entire squad using a scrub he relished the opportunity.

Skip Plotnicki officially became the first Tennessee basketball player to be reprimanded by Coach Mears in practice and became a human sacrifice. The message was clear to all the Volunteer players.

Skip went on to a rather non-descript career at UT, but despite some setbacks he did "go the distance" in Coach Mears' program and graduated. During his years at Tennessee he had a lot of wonderful teammates that created a multitude of life-long memories. Over the years these players have remained a closeknit group, sharing moments of joy in successes and comforting each other in times of grief. Playing for the Head Vol had a way of bonding all of them together. Many values of Coach's program were not measured in conference championships or individual greatness; many benefits lasted a lifetime.

Beware of Your Next Door Neighbor

The Volunteer Basketball Team in Blacksburg, Virginia, for a contest was preparing to check out of their motel rooms. Skip Plotnicki and Pat Robinette roomed together on the road and their accommodations were next to Haywood Harris, UT Sports Information Director. There was a door that connected the adjoining rooms and it was unlocked, giving Plotnicki and Robinette access to Haywood's room.

Haywood had his back turned away from the door and was finishing the packing of his suitcase. Noticing an opportunity to bring a man to his senses, Pat Robinette quietly approached Haywood, stood behind him, and let out a blood-curdling scream. Haywood fell directly onto the bed in a state of terror, trembling from head to toe and fearing for his life. Mustering the courage to turn around, he saw Robinette grinning from ear to ear. "Robinette, I just got my dream job as sports director at Tennessee and you almost gave me a heart attack," the startled Harris exclaimed.

As a result of this caper, Coach Mears delegated Haywood the job of setting up away game room assignments. He made absolutely sure that Robinette and Plotnicki were housed as far from his room as possible.

A couple of years ago Pat and Skip were playing in the T-Club Golf Tournament when they spotted Gus Manning and Haywood Harris. They stopped the duo and had a short conversation. As Plotnicki and Robinette drove their golf cart away, Pat jokingly asked Haywood, "Where're you sleeping tonight?" To which Haywood replied, "I'm damn sure not telling you!"

After almost forty years, Haywood Harris still remembered the day he almost became the shortest term Tennessee Sports Information Director in history as a result of a practical joke by one of Ray's boys, Pat Robinette.

Anyone Seen This Photo?

It was springtime on the UT campus, a time for the UT basketball fraternity to take a much-deserved rest. Some players went home to visit with their family while others journeyed to Florida to soak up the rays. For most students the UT Aquatic Center was a popular place during the pre-summer afternoons. Basketball players and others customarily coated their bodies with baby oil and relaxed by the water, conferring with girlfriends and best buddies.

One hot afternoon Marty Morris, a Vol assistant basketball coach, showed up at the Center with a photographer to shoot some pictures of some of the players for the basketball recruiting brochure. A lot of the pictures taken were of players with their girlfriends lounging around the pool, and I was there enjoying the spring break with my future wife Debbie.

Coach Morris motioned for us to come over and I assumed he was going to take a picture of Debbie and me. He instructed me to get into the water where a portable basketball goal was stationed Assuming Debbie was following me, I entered the pool. The next thing I knew Coach Morris was directing a bikini clad model into the water and he instructed her to get on my shoulders so she could shoot a ball into the goal while being photographed. Although somewhat embarrassed by the situation but being ordered by the coach, I stayed put and finished the photo session. When I got out of the pool, Debbie was nowhere to be found; her friend told me that she was quite upset and had left.

Later that afternoon I went to Coach Morris' office to ask if he would call Debbie and explain the situation. He did phone her and she gave him an "ear-cleaning." She had not cooled off at all. Coach Morris apologized and informed her he would not use the picture. In fact, he said that he would destroy the photo and the negative.

Deb thought the matter was resolved until a few years later. While she was working for the Bank of Maryville, A. W. Davis, who at the time was a UT assistant coach, stopped in to see his good friend Kenny Coulter who was Debbie's boss.

A. W. spoke to Deb and told her that he had a picture she might be interested in. He opened a file folder and there it was—the infamous pool photo that Marty Morris had promised to destroy. Kenny, A.W. and Deb all had a good laugh reminiscing the event. Even though Marty Morris was not present, he received another tongue-lashing from Deb for old time's sake.

As A. W. started to leave, Deb, reminding him of his offer, said, "Coach Davis, you forgot to give me something." A. W. responded, "This picture belongs to the UT Sports Information Department and they have the rights to it; you'll have to talk to them."

How Do You Get an Orange to the Big Apple?

In 1971 the Tennessee Vols were invited to participate in the National Invitational Tournament in New York City. The classic was to be played in Madison Square Garden, known as the mecca of basketball. The team's first round opponent was St. Johns, an eastern powerhouse and one of the toughest squads in the tournament.

Although St. Johns was a stiff assignment, the real challenge came not from a foe on the court but a decision the Tennessee staff had to make. Traditionally, during the home games a giant orange mascot danced around the court entertaining the fans. It was the same orange mascot Coach Aberdeen stationed himself in to watch a Vol game during the 1969-70 season due to sickness.

The dilemma was: How do you get the big orange to the big apple? A couple of suggestions were made: (1) You could slice the orange into four pieces and ship it in a crate on the plane but piecing it back together could prove to be difficult; or (2) you could leave it at Knoxville but that would be a break from tradition and, according to the superstitious Coach Mears, could result in bad luck.

The final solution came when Coach Mears and his staff decided to rent a large U-haul-it truck which could barely fit the orange mascot in its premises and have the manager drive it non-stop to New York. To make sure unexpected obstacles would be overcome along the way, Mears had one of his graduate assistant coaches help in escorting the large fruit.

The orange made it to New York and when it was not performing in the pre-game activities it rested in the cramped quarters of the truck, sapping up rental money without activity. The Vols beat St Johns but lost to Duke in the second round so neither the orange mascot nor its drivers got much rest before they had to make the long journey back to Knoxville.

Don't Break the Circle

 During the Ray Mears basketball era, team unity and togetherness was a top priority. There was not room for prima donnas (the words describing players who thought more of themselves than the team). Volunteer roundballers were conditioned to respect each other and play as a unit.

Coach Aberdeen had the ultimate togetherness drill in his pre-season program. When most squads took a break from strenuous conditioning drills, they might rest by sitting on a chair replenishing lost fluids with water, but "Beef" had another regimen for his troops: After fifteen minutes of heart wrenching fitness drills, he would blow his whistle and all twelve to fourteen players would dreadfully head to the small circle located in the center of the court. They were to remain in the small circumference for two minutes, and it was considered a violation if any body parts exceeded the perimeter.

Players clung to each other like their life depended on it. They were thirsty and tired but to prove they were one unit they attempted to stay in the circle. Every once in a while someone's toe would edge outside the premises but not for long as Aberdeen would quickly step on the appendage.

Togetherness might be one thing but the most rewarding part of the drill was its conclusion when one could again breathe and rid himself of teammates' sweat and body odor. Fresh air could be exhilarating even if you had another fifteen minutes of agilities before returning to the circle.

Best Advice—No Advice

When Bernard King arrived on the UT campus, Coach Mears had heard from reliable sources that the prize recruit "could do it all" but his mid range jump shot was a "little suspect." During an early season practice session, the Vol mentor instructed Coach A. W. Davis, who had been an outstanding Volunteer shooter, to tutor the young Vol in the art of shooting proficiency.

Taking the inside New Yorker to a side goal, Coach Davis, for the purpose of evaluating his shooting style, asked Bernard to attempt a few shots. Then he proceeded to instruct him on hand placement of the ball; squaring to the basket; hand, arm, elbow, and shoulder alignment; and proper release of the ball. "Always keep your eye on the target—the basket," A.W. stressed.

While reviewing the shooting fundamentals, Coach Davis noticed that "B" had little eye contact with him and he seemed to be bored and inattentive with the instruction. Realizing Bernard had heard enough, he motioned for the inside "phenom" to take a few more shots.

Much to Coach Davis' disappointment, "B" did not make any shooting technique adjustments. He also did not miss many shots as one ball after another rippled the nets. With a look of disbelief A. W. propped himself up next to the goal post and watched Bernard put on a shooting clinic, hitting on a percentage of shots that was close to perfection.

After approximately thirty minutes of non-stop shooting, Coach Mears motioned for Bernard to enter the team scrimmage. "B's" shooting expertise continued as each shot seemed to hit its mark through the goal, and he seemed to enjoy impressing the coaches with his exceptional talent.

Upon witnessing this display of extraordinary shooting accuracy, Coach Mears summoned the team to mid court and asked A.W. to step forward. He told the former Vol All American that he had done a great job in assisting Bernard in perfecting his shooting and that he had never seen any player improve so quickly in such a short period of time.

As the scrimmage resumed A. W. just went back to leaning against the side goal post, thinking to himself, "Best advice is sometimes no advice."

Circus-Day Parade

Oh! the Circus-day Parade! How the bugles played and played!
And how the glossy horses tossed their flossy manes and neighed,
As the rattle and the rhyme of the tenor-drummer's time
Filled all the hungry hearts of us with melody sublime!

How the grand band-wagon shone with a splendor all its own,
And glittered with a glory that our dreams had never known!
And how the boys behind, high and low of every kind,
Marched in unconscious capture, with a rapture undefined!

The horsemen, two and two, with their plumes of white and blue
And crimson, gold and purple, nodding by at me and you,
Waved the banners that they bore, as the knights in days of yore,
Till our glad eyes gleamed and glistened like the spangles that they wore!

How the graceless-graceful stride of the elephant was eyed,
And the capers of the little horse that cantered at his side!
How the shambling camels, tame to the plaudits of their fame,
With listless eyes came silent, masticating as they came.

How the cages jolted past, with each wagon battened fast,
And the mystery within it only hinted of at last
From the little grated square in the rear, and nosing there
The snout of some strange animal that sniffed the outer air!

And, last of all, the Clown, making mirth for all the town,
With his lips curved ever upward and his eyebrows ever down,
And his chief attention paid to the little mule that played
A tattoo on the dashboard with his heels in the Parade.

Oh! The Circus-Day Parade! How the bugles played and played!
And how the glossy horses tossed their flossy manes and neighed,
As the rattle and the rhyme of the tenor-drummer's time
Filled all the hungry hearts of us with melody sublime!

James Whitcomb Riley
The Hoosier Poet

Afterword

During the Ray Mears Era there have been hundreds of stories told, maybe even thousands, and to put them all in a book would have been an impossible endeavor. With this project I have only tipped the iceberg. Throughout my life stories have always been an inspiration to me. There is nothing I like better on a daily basis than a good story; they make my day and make life more tolerable.

If a story in this book has brought back a memory, put a tear in your eye, convinced you just how old you are getting, or brought a smile to your face, then all the effort that went into its production will have been worthwhile. It does not take me very long to enter Thompson-Boling Arena today and see that the atmosphere has changed in thirty years. Marketing people might try to create hoopla, coaches might wear orange blazers, music might be played over the loud speakers, cheerleaders might perform acrobatic stunts, jumbo screens might try to excite, but it is just not like life under the big top during the Ray Mears Era.

For the people that experienced the games in Stokely Athletic Center I have a suggestion. When you attend the contests in Thompson Boling Arena, try to do as I do. When all the pre-game festivities are occurring, casually look up at the banners hanging from the rafters representing the Ray Mears Era, close your eyes and you just might see the Tennessee Vol pep band marching around the court, the cheerleaders shaking their orange and white pompoms, the proud Vols performing their colorful Globetrotter antics, Ray Mears with his arms across his chest watching his Vols warm up, Stu Aberdeen displaying his sideline gyrations, the Vols running through the gigantic orange T, or Ernie and Bernie putting on a show. Then sadly, the moment of illusions will certainly be short-lived and with their fading, as with all memories, one should just forget the scores and remember the stories.

A Tribute to Coach Ray Mears

Bill Justus

Coach Ray Mears was an innovator, a competitor, an entertainer, and a coaching genius. He was well ahead of his time in the use of a point guard (one guard front), spread offense (four corners), clock management, insistence on using each player's special skills, and countless other details in the game of basketball.

But for his former players, his most lasting contribution to us came in the form of life's lessons taught: Prepare well, practice self-discipline, outwork the competition, continue to develop your strengths (and turn to them in a crisis), and remember, "It only costs a little more to go first class."

Coach Ray Mears' contributions to Tennessee basketball are legendary and well documented. He belongs in the College Basketball Hall of Fame. On a more silent front, his importance in the development of his former players is even more notable—strong, solid lessons learned while crossing that fragile precipice from boyhood to manhood; there is no way to assign a value to those teachings.

It was all part of a great college experience as Tennessee basketball players. Without Coach Ray Mears that experience would have been greatly diminished.

Billy Justus, Captain, UT Basketball Vols, 1969

Year-by-Year Record of Coach Mears at Tennessee

SEC Coach of the Year

1967 Ray Mears
(AP, UPI, *Knoxville News-Sentinel)*

1977 Ray Mears
(AP, UPI, *Knoxville News-Sentinel)*

1962-63	13-11
1963-64	16-8
1964-65	20-5
1964-65	18-8
1966-67	21-7
1967-68	20-6
1968-69	21-7
1969-70	16-9
1970-71	21-7
1971-72	19-6
1972-73	15-9
1973-74	17-9
1974-75	18-8
1975-76	21-6
1976-77	22-6
15 years	278-112	.713 Pct.

About the Author

Mike Edwards

Mike Edwards grew up in the basketball-rich state of Indiana, learning the game on the playgrounds and boys' club in his hometown of Greenfield, Indiana. The Hoosier native made his mark on the central Indiana hardwood. Coached by Indianapolis Tech and Purdue standout, Mel Garland, and Joe Stanley, Edwards attained an amazing 2,343 points during his high school career. This accomplishment presently ranks him seventh in the overall Indiana scores list. He led the state in points in 1969 (36.4 average) and was the state's second leading scorer in 1968 (32.0 average). His shooting prowess earned him All State and All American honors his senior year along with a selection to the prestigious Indiana All Star Team.

Edwards' accolades did not end on the high school level but followed him to the University of Tennessee where he played for Ray Mears. Nicknamed the "Greenfield Gunner," he helped lead the Vols to the NIT in 1971 and a SEC Co-Championship in

1972. Edwards was named to the All SEC Team in 1972 and again in 1973. He was voted the SEC Player of the Year in 1972 by the UPI. The "Greenfield Gunner" averaged 30.1 points per game on the Tennessee Freshmen Team, and he finished his varsity college career with 1,343 points before the three-point shot was initiated. He was an Academic All SEC in 1971-72-73 and an Academic All American in 1972. Edwards was drafted by the Indiana Pacers and played basketball professionally in Mexico.

Mike spent sixteen years coaching basketball on both the high school and college levels. In 1994 he was elected to the Indiana Basketball Hall of Fame Silver Anniversary Team, and in 2003 he obtained the ultimate honor for all Hoosier roundballers—induction into the Indiana Basketball Hall of Fame.

Edwards resides in Maryville, Tennessee, along with his wife of over thirty years Debbie. Both are schoolteachers.

Don't Give Me the Scores, Just the Stories is Mike's second book. *The Last Tiger, an Indiana Basketball Story,* his first book, was published in 1995.

Printed in the United States
41429LVS00004B/40-45